Dr. Lee Ann B. Marino, Ph.D., D.Min., D.D.

Most
Blessed

Among All Women

MOST BLESSED

Among All Women

DR. LEE ANN B. MARINO, PH.D., D.MIN., D.D.

Published by:
PHOTINI PRESS
(an imprint of The Righteous Pen Publications Group)
www.righteouspenpublications.com

Unless otherwise noted, Scriptures taken from the Holy Bible, New International Version®, NIV®, Copyright © 1973, 1978, 1984, 2011 by Biblica, Inc. ™ Used by permission of Zondervan. All rights reserved worldwide.

Passages marked EXB taken from the Expanded Bible. Copyright 2011 by Thomas Nelson, Inc. Used by permission. All rights reserved.

Passages marked KJV taken from the Authorized King James Version of the Holy Bible, Public Domain.

Scriptures marked GW are a copyrighted work of *God's Word to the Nations*. Quotations are used by permission. Copyright 1995 by God's Word to the Nations. All rights reserved.

Scriptures marked AMPC are taken from the Amplified® Bible, Classic Edition Copyright © 1954, 1958, 1962, 1964, 1965, 1987 by The Lockman Foundation. Used by permission." (www.Lockman.org)

I Am A Warring Woman appearing in Chapter 3 and *The Song of the Strong Woman* appearing in Chapter 8 are © 2011 by the author.

Cover photo Atahan Demir, interior photo Heber Vasquez, pexels.com

Book classification:
1. Nonfiction > Religion > Christian Life > Women's Issues.

Copyright © 2017, 2025 by Lee Ann B. Marino.

ISBN: 1-940197-40-6
13-Digit: 978-1-940197-40-1

Printed in the United States of America.

O my God
teach my heart where and how to seek You,
where and how to find You...

You are my God and You are my All
and I have never seen You.
You have made me and remade me,
You have bestowed on me all the good things I possess,
Still I do not know You...

I have not yet done that for which I was made...
Teach me to seek You...

I cannot seek You unless You teach me
or find You unless You show Yourself to me.
Let me seek You in my desire,
let me desire You in my seeking.
Let me find You by loving You,
let me love You when I find You.

(Anselm of Canterbury)

TABLE OF CONTENTS

ACKNOWLEDGEMENTS

I N writing this book, I sincerely acknowledge and thank each and every woman I have had the honor of knowing and working with in ministry. Some situations have turned out terrible and others turned out great, but regardless of the outcome, I am blessed for the journey. We only come to learn some things by experience. This this book is not just the result of research, but true experience. I know it was only obtainable if I took that step and experienced life and ministry with other women who have made the same commitment I have: to serve, live, and preach the Gospel throughout life. This book is about us, for us, and dedicated to us.

INTRODUCTION

"Most Blessed Among All Women"

WRITING a book is always a big undertaking. It is an even bigger undertaking when you juggle multiple writing projects at once. This is the state I find myself in as I write these words. I am about five chapters in on a book specifically for men, about halfway done with a magazine that we have due out for my publishing company in about three weeks, and a few other assorted tasks here and there, including several handbooks and manuals for organizations. It wasn't time to take on a new project, at least within my mind. I like to finish what I am doing when I start it, thus I intended to finish the magazine, finish the book for men, and then maybe...just maybe...think about doing something new. Yet...here I am. For the past two days, I have had thoughts and promptings to start working on this book, so I am starting it, and waiting to see where it will take me. All the books I write are a journey, and it is always interesting to see where I wind up.

My original idea for *Most Blessed Among All Women* was a sermon series I constructed way back in 2009. After that, it was an idea for a conference theme. I never wound up preaching the message and we never wound up using the conference theme (at least to date). When I talked about it as a conference theme people would get excited about it, but we never seemed to get it together enough to use it as a theme for the grand event we hoped to have. Like so many other things, with the passage of time, we forgot about it and moved forward.

One day in late 2015 God brought the conference theme back into full focus when I gave a woman formerly covered by our ministry the message that she was "most blessed among women." It was confirmation for her of another word the Lord already gave to her. When I mentioned it was a sermon I'd put together, she asked me "Where is the book on it?" I was already writing a book and wasn't thinking about writing a new one, but something about her words made me think. I went and dug up my old sermon notes (which were typed and quite detailed back then) and put the binder in full view so I would be sure to get *Most Blessed Among All Women* written after the start of the new year.

Many long and detailed things changed between the first view of this as a book and where I sit today. One writing project led to another, and I didn't start the book I wanted to when I wanted to do it. I had other projects to finish and other books that were closer to completion, so I made *Most Blessed Among All Women* wait. I also, due to some of my own decisions, felt it was best to work on women's ministry in a different way than I had been doing for the past several years. It was just time to do something different. The way I had been doing things was not making me feel "most blessed," or blessed at all. I no longer wanted to work with other women or even talk to them. I disliked how I was treated, and I found the behavior of so many in ministry to be nothing more than aggravating.

It's easy to look out over the landscape of social and even ministerial relationships we have with other women and want to give up on them all together. I think it's more tempting to want to absorb what men tell us about ourselves from the pulpit and believe it. It's even more tempting to read the Bible and look at the women therein with rose-colored glasses, believing they had no problems or issues in their lives and that being "most blessed" means sitting under a glass cake stand somewhere as angels play *How Great Thou Art* within listening distance.

Being "most blessed," however, doesn't quite have the connotation we might like it to have. It doesn't mean we have the most money and can walk into a room, turning all attention to ourselves, all the time. It doesn't mean showing all other women up, nor does it mean that life is perfect. It is a relatively simple idea that means what we do outlasts us and others recognize us for exactly what we are as God leads us and the contributions we make. It is a celebration of who we are, of the beauty that rests upon being a woman and thinking like one, and the joy of excitement as God works in and through us, one moment and step at a time.

Come along with me and let's learn about these Biblical women – some well-known, some rather unknown – and what made them special, just as we also learn what makes us special and unique before God. Through this book, may we each gain greater insight into how and why God blesses us, and why we too can rise up and sing that we are "most blessed."

CHAPTER ONE

What it Means to be
"Most Blessed Among All Women"

*YOUR BEAUTY SHOULD NOT COME FROM OUTWARD ADORNMENT, SUCH AS
ELABORATE HAIRSTYLES AND THE WEARING OF GOLD JEWELRY OR FINE CLOTHES.
RATHER, IT SHOULD BE THAT OF YOUR INNER SELF, THE UNFADING BEAUTY OF
A GENTLE AND QUIET SPIRIT, WHICH IS OF GREAT WORTH IN GOD'S SIGHT.
FOR THIS IS THE WAY THE HOLY WOMEN OF THE PAST WHO PUT THEIR HOPE
IN GOD USED TO ADORN THEMSELVES...*
(1 PETER 3:3-5)

WHEN I grew up in the Catholic Church, saying a woman was "most blessed among all women" was reserved for one woman alone: Mary, the mother of Jesus. If any of us had claimed that term for ourselves, we would have been accused of blasphemy, put on detention, and forced to do some sort of report on Mary and why the Catholic Church esteemed her in the way it did.

I took this mentality into my adult years, long after I left the Catholic Church. It never crossed my mind that anyone else was blessed in the same way Mary was, and I never called myself most blessed or thought of myself in that way. This was up until several years ago (so many I can't remember exactly who said it to me), when I had a bunch of email pen pals (there to exchange emails back and forth). It was common for us to talk about the Bible and things of faith, as most of us were Christians. One was a young man who I did not know very well, nor did I talk to him for very long, as we lost contact after only a few correspondences. In one email, he ended it with a line that has stayed with me all these years: "Until next time, stay most blessed among all women!"

I'd never, ever thought about applying that promise beyond Mary because I never thought much about what it meant or why Mary received that word. Most of us can remember where Mary proclaimed herself "most blessed among all women" (and yes, we will look at this passage in this book). The "why" Mary was called as such is just as important as the "who," and it gives us all an important and special perspective on what it means to be blessed, what it means to be among all women, and how God relates to us as women and the choices we must make, right where we are.

Saying "Yes" To God

I meet a lot of women today who believe they are called to ministry. I have come, through many years of ministry myself, to believe this is both a good thing and a bad thing. It is a good thing because I know that God does call women to ministry, and I am encouraged to see women who are genuinely called of God pursue what He calls them to do. I think it's bad because we now have the impression that the only way to serve God or to say "yes" to God is to be in ministry. This has caused a virtual flood on the ministry scene. With so many people (including and especially women) clamoring to get into the pulpit, the focus of ministry is rapidly changing. I meet many women who seek ordination as a validation for the suffering or difficulties of their lives. I also meet many women who use ministry as a substitution for personal validation or to try and work out their own healing and issues. Instead of working out the issues that we all, not just as women, but as people have – rejection, hurt, anger, injustice, and self-worth – they are taking these issues into the pulpit and following suit with vanity and egocentrism. The results are ministries often disordered and chaotic, because their leaders have difficulty staying focused on ministry. Their personal lives ultimately overtake ministry aspirations.

Don't get me wrong. I think being in ministry is a wonderful thing if that is genuinely what God has called you to do. If you are genuinely called to ministry, then you need to get training to learn how to balance the difficulties of life and home along with ministry vision. If it's not what you are called to do, then I think it's misleading and problematic. Contrary to popular belief, it is all right to not be called to ministry. You can still serve God and find your center as "most blessed." Not being in ministry doesn't mean you serve God any less or that you are any less important in His sight. It just means you aren't in ministry.

I think we assume saying "yes' to God means having to do something big and grand on a large scale. We assume this because we associate the grand gestures and stages we often see in large ministries as the only way we can, as people, serve God. We are also told if we want to be blessed by God, we must be "outrageous givers," which is usually associated with giving large sums of money to the minister who tells us to be givers. In our minds, that becomes it. If we want to tell God "yes" to His call for our lives, we think that means having a huge, internationally-known ministry or giving a lot of money to someone who does. Nothing else, no middle ground, nada.

Saying "yes" to God means accepting God's plan for your life, not fitting into the will of someone else's wallet or concept of life's success. What I love about this study into the women who were called "most blessed" in the Bible is seeing that they were women who did the extraordinary with their own lives, walking as they were supposed to, with the grace and ease of God upon them. They said yes to Him, not to everyone else around them or to what was popular or conventional at the time. This means that it was Mary's "yes" (and the other women's) to God that rendered her (and them) "Most blessed along all women." If all it takes is our simple "yes" – to live as He calls us to

7

live (which is far more than just writing out and following a church code) and walk as He calls us to walk – to be most blessed, then we, too, can be "most blessed" among all women.

Having the "right spirit"

We talk a lot today about having the Spirit or "getting the Spirit." The reality is that the Holy Ghost, the Holy Spirit, as we often call Him, is always here, and is always with us, no matter who or what is around us. We choose whether we allow the Spirit to overtake our lives and lead us into places that are blessed and fruitful. We can also choose to be led by things that are destructive and bothersome. Even though it is seldom spoken of like this, allowing the Spirit to work in our lives – or not – is very much a choice. We choose who we follow, and if we choose to follow the flesh, our own selfish desires, or the enemy, all of that becomes a willful, deliberate choice at some point in time.

It doesn't help that the emotional fervor climate present in the church is often taught to be the Spirit of God when it's not. We tend to associate intense emotional states, stirrings, and strong feelings with God, when it can just as often be the opposite of God. Just because you have a feeling, a thought, an idea, a conviction, or an idea doesn't mean that you should run wild with it, here and there, cursing out the devil or spinning yourself into a stressed state.

The Spirit of God does not operate by crazy, insane emotional outbursts. It's fine to be excited about what God does (and it's awesome to display that enthusiasm), but it is not fine to think emotional fervor dictates where God moves. Just because someone is irate or bursting forth with feelings all the time doesn't mean that they have the Spirit of God within them or that they are moved by that Spirit.

Being blessed means you have God's Spirit within you, and you can endure and handle anything that comes along, no matter how difficult or off-putting it might seem to be. We talk much about warfare, but I have genuinely come to find the best warfare tactics are those that come about when we are focused and not easily thrown off course by everything that comes along. In the spiritual life, we are going to deal with warfare, but how much warfare comes our way depends on how we handle it. Some people just seem to keep going through and through and through again because they don't learn how to handle things, and thus, they block the blessed life that God desires them to have.

All the women we are going to look at in this book fall into the category of being "strategists." They were women who knew how to act and how to handle the things that came against them. If anything, they were women who knew how to handle their emotions, their emotional states, and knew when to act and when not to act. This rendered them blessed because they knew that a blessed life didn't mean a life without stress or frustration, but that when such things came up, they would be given the strategy to deal with the enemy and move forward in God, blessed and content.

What does it mean to be "blessed?"

The Amplified Bible, Classic Edition amplifies the word "blessed" with the words "Blessed, happy, fortunate, to be envied." This is a great extended definition of what it means to be blessed, because it gives us the clear indication that being blessed is a state of being full to overflowing of God's joy and grace upon us. *Strong's Exhaustive Concordance of the Bible* defines the Greek word as *makarios*, meaning "Blessed, happy."[1] This means those who are blessed have something special about them, a divine marking, a distinction that renders them happy, fortunate, and enviable by others.

Don't we want to be blessed? Don't we want to have this in our lives? What we don't recognize is that being blessed is something God wants us to have in our lives because it marks His intervention therein. It is not His will that we live in misery, moving from thing to thing and service to service, chasing a preacher to give us insight into why we keep living the same patterns over and over again. Blessing breaks the cycles that we have lived with for too many years, and the reason it does this is because being blessed is a witness. In order to get blessed, we have to do something radical in our witness. With that witness comes a testimony, and with that testimony comes the insight into how – and why – God has moved in such a powerful way in our lives.

Becoming blessed

In the following chapters, we are going to look at seven women that the Bible called "Most blessed:" Mary, Jael, Eve, The Song of Solomon Woman, the Proverbs 31 woman, the barren woman, and the Christian woman. Each of these women is special in her own right, with her own story that may, in many ways, sounds like your own story, or your own struggle. In their own walk to be blessed, we are going to see the choices they made, the difficulties they faced, the ways that being blessed set them apart and challenged their times and challenged their relationship with everything they thought they knew about God.

If we want the same, we must prepare ourselves for the same: to be different, to be challenged, to face difficulties, and to have our relationship with God change. Are you ready for the journey? God is calling, so let's go!

CHAPTER TWO

Mary
- Her Soul Magnifies the Lord -

HIS MOTHER SAID TO THE SERVANTS, "DO WHATEVER HE TELLS YOU."
(JOHN 2:5)

WHAT were you doing when you were 12 or 13 years old? If you were anything like I was at that age, you were in junior high, trying to survive. Life was confusing and difficult. Our current crush was interested one day, then not interested the next. School, parents, and teachers all seemed impossible. We were the oldest we had ever been, yet not old enough to do so much that seemed just out of our reach. We were worried about pimples, school dances, passing grades, hanging out with friends, and figuring out life, which seemed large and intimidating...yet confining and constricting, all at the same time. Marriage, families, babies, the rest of our lives, even college (or high school, on some days) seemed a long way off.

Mary, mother of Jesus, wasn't afforded the luxury adolescence most of us experienced as young women. By the time she was 12 or 13 years old, she was betrothed to be married and had an angelic encounter, telling her she would become the mother of the Savior. Her life experience was very far from our own at that age, but her encounter with God is one that changed the course of human history and our own experiences with God, forever. Even though she might have started her process much younger and with far more fervor than most of us did, we can learn a lot from Mary and see ourselves in her and her experience as a woman who was declared "most blessed."

Mary is very, very important for us as Christian women. She is not important in the sense of being a goddess or worshiping her as a false deity. We cannot deny, however, that Mary is extremely important in the proclamation of the Gospel message and walked a very difficult road, full of testimony, as she answered God's call to become the mother of the Savior.

Women in Mary's time

In Matthew 1, there are only five women mentioned in the genealogy of Jesus. Most scholars brush this fact aside. The fact, however, that these women are mentioned there – most of whom were Gentile (non-Jewish) women – is most relevant. They weren't there to take up space and look cute. Their inclusion was not a side point, something to consider as a secondary factor. They were history makers, revolutionary women, also blessed in all they did because they paved the way for salvation.

Matthew 1:3,5,16:

Judah the father of Perez and Zerah, whose mother was Tamar...Salmon the father of Boaz, whose mother was Rahab, Boaz the father of Obed, whose mother was Ruth...David was the father of Solomon, whose mother had been Uriah's wife...and Jacob the father of Joseph, the husband of Mary, and Mary was the mother of Jesus Who is called the Messiah.

Tamar, Rahab, Ruth, Bathsheba, and Mary are all mentioned as part of the lineage of Jesus. Mary was the wife of Joseph and the mother of Jesus. Before we learn anything else about Mary, we learn there was something special about her. Mary wasn't just another woman, just another cog in the wheel, even though her culture destined her to such.

In Mary's time, women didn't exist for any other purpose but to bear children, specifically male heirs. Women were regarded as the personal property of their husbands, acquired through business transactions. Even though there were women who did work and operate businesses (such as Lydia, mentioned in Acts 16:14) and women certainly contributed to the upkeep of society through farming, herding, and other agricultural duties, they received little to no credit for any sort of contribution to society.

Women were married very young through family arrangements. Betrothals were often discussed while girls were still children and solidified as soon as they hit puberty. Within a month of a girl's first menstrual cycle, she was considered a woman and ready for marriage. Duty – a cement of clan culture – was a must from the first day of marriage.

Think this is appalling and scary at the same time? Consider these girls had no part in their marriage arrangements. Marriage was considered business. It wasn't about love, friendship, romance, spirituality, or even something with much religious attachment (save ceremonies did become religious in nature). The marriage "deal" was made between the father or oldest male relative and the family of her betrothed, by which there would be the exchange of the girl for goods (such as money, cattle, or work). The deal was sealed with a ring or other expensive item.

Girls were regarded as a burden on their families of birth. They didn't carry their father's name after marriage, and they were not to inherit property if their father died. This means if she had no brothers, family property would become the property of her husband and his family rather than remaining in her family. If a girl never married by bringing disgrace to her family or if she was, for some reason, divorced by her husband, she would become a life-long financial burden on her family. Thus, there was a great push to arrange marriages for female daughters as soon as the option became feasible. The suitor who offered the best deal for his daughter was the only choice. No consideration was made for how a man might treat his wife, if he was a suitable provider, or if he was given to bad habits or dishonesty. The goal was to get rid of her as soon as possible for the best price obtainable.

After the business arrangements were made, girls were subject to long periods of betrothal to give young brides time to get used to the idea of marriage and having children. They were given little to no information about sex. In fact, virgin brides were prized as men wanted to ensure male heirs were theirs, and theirs alone. The men were usually a good ten or more years older than the girls, and they had little contact with their future brides before the year prior to the wedding.

In the final year betrothal period prior to the wedding, there would be a period where the young girl would move into the male's family home, and they would live as husband and wife in every aspect except they did not sexually consummate their relationship. If the man died during this time, the woman was considered a widow. If the woman died, he was free to marry again. The man also had the option to leave the woman in this period for any reason, and she would be considered divorced.

Before we write off the first century as an appalling place, it's important to remember that customs surrounding marriage and family have changed throughout history. What might seem unfathomable today wasn't at earlier points in time, because society deemed relationships, genders, and identities differently than we do now. We don't study the past to judge it, but to understand better the stage set as God moved among people, even back then.

Young Jewish women in the first century prayed daily to God, that if it be His will, they might become the mother of the Messiah, the One Who would come and liberate God's people. I would venture it was a prayer that had been spoken so many times before, Mary probably didn't think twice about saying it. It was something said in tradition, recited repeatedly, by requirement. Yet Mary said it, as a young woman, and found its fulfillment in her young life, one that up until that point in time, she probably didn't expect to be very extraordinary.

Enter Mary

Mary, the mother of Jesus, was born into the world we just discussed. It was void of personal choice, consideration for her as a person, and of her own opinion. She was going through the motions of her life, a life that was not her own. She lived with the expectations of other people, the anticipations of what life was supposed to become for her, and she probably experienced intense anxiety about doing things "just so" according to custom.

Then God shook up her world in a way that only God can do.

Luke 1:26-35:

In the sixth month of Elizabeth's pregnancy, God sent the angel Gabriel to Nazareth, a town in Galilee, to a virgin pledged to be married to a man named Joseph, a descendant of David. The virgin's name was Mary. The angel went to her and said, "Greetings, you who are highly favored! The Lord is with you."

Mary was greatly troubled at his words and wondered what kind of greeting this might be. But the angel said to her, "Do not be afraid, Mary; you have found favor with God. You will conceive and give birth to a Son, and you are to call Him Jesus. He will be great and will be called the Son of the Most High. The Lord God will give Him the throne of His father David, and He will reign over Jacob's descendants forever; His Kingdom will never end."

"How will this be," Mary asked the angel, "since I am a virgin?"

The angel answered, "The Holy Spirit will come on you, and the power of the Most High will overshadow you. So the Holy One to be born will be called the Son of God."

BLESSED THOUGHTS:

Why mercy triumphs over judgment

For to him who has shown no mercy the judgment [will be] merciless, but mercy [full of glad confidence] exults victoriously over judgment. (James 2:13, AMPC)

Maybe she was lonely. Maybe she was a battered wife, abused and abandoned by her husband. Maybe her husband had left her. Maybe she was trying to make money (there was no "unemployment office" back then). Maybe her husband was also cheating on her. Maybe she didn't know who she was. Maybe she felt unloved. Maybe she wanted more in her life and thought she would find it in a man. Maybe she thought he really loved her. Maybe she thought she'd found 'the one' and didn't know where to start with it in her life. Maybe she wanted some excitement and didn't think she'd get caught. Maybe she was unloved. Maybe she wanted to get caught. Maybe she wanted out. Maybe a part of her just wanted to die.

Maybe it doesn't matter what the 'maybe' was because we aren't meant to know. Maybe all that matters is that God knew, and we don't. Maybe, just maybe, that is relevant.

All the people around her had opinions about her and what she had done. They looked down on her, and thought she deserved to die for what she did. It didn't matter that they did things every day and were sneaky enough to not get caught. Not to mention, the vast number of people who knew what they did but looked the other way because of who was doing various things. Behind closed doors, every one of them either did the same things, did different things, or thought about doing those things. Somebody envied her. Somebody imagined what she did and longed for those moments she had. Somebody wanted to pelt the rocks hard and fast because they longed to do what she did but couldn't bring themselves to do it. Somebody hated her. Somebody looked at her and saw everything wrong in the world. Somebody blamed her for everything that was wrong with society. Somebody called her names. Somebody talked about her behind her back. They caught wind of what was going on and told everyone they could find, but told everyone they told to "keep it a secret." We all know they went on and talked, too.

Somebody mocked her. Somebody felt they had the right to wish death upon her. Somebody was there, ready to fling that stone, because they were better than her.

The woman caught in adultery (John 8:1-11) reveals something essential to us about the Christian life and especially something essential for those called to leadership. I call it non-judgment. Non-judgment is a principle by which we choose to be merciful, recognizing who we are and not using what others have done against them, to make ourselves feel better. Whether we like to admit it or not, judgment makes us feel good about ourselves. It makes us feel more acceptable to God considering what we do and look down upon people for falling into what they have done. It's a comfortable place, a cushy place, a place where black and white and right and wrong stare in a punitive, cold, unmerciful accusation where what should be right and should be ideal is used as a weapon.

The story of the woman caught in adultery, therefore, is very important. In some ways, it reminds me of the accusations made against Mary when she was found to be pregnant with Jesus (Matthew 1:18-19). The people of Mary's day didn't view her any differently than they viewed this woman. She was unmarried, she was pregnant, Joseph was not claiming to be the father, and as far as they were concerned, her pregnancy was the evidence they needed. Pregnant by the Holy Spirit with the Son of God? A big yeah right, get real. Nobody believed her. She could have told the truth, and nobody would have listened. She could have implored, but it wouldn't have mattered. Instead, we do not see Mary speak in her own defense. It wouldn't have changed their sanctimonious self-righteousness disguised as upholding a godly principle. It wouldn't make them understand what she was going through or what her life was going to be like. Nobody would have cared about the reality of the task God set before her. It wasn't going to be manger scenes as the "holy family" sat around the campfire and sang *Kumbaya*. She didn't speak because it didn't matter.

The Bible doesn't indicate the woman caught in adultery spoke, either. There wasn't any reason to speak. It wasn't going to matter what she said, they wouldn't believe her, anyway. It wouldn't change their minds. It wouldn't change their minds. It wouldn't change their hearts.

I wonder if there is another reason for their silence, a deeper reason, an introspective reason. I wonder if somewhere behind the silence both Mary and the woman caught in adultery remembered all the thoughts and accusations they made about others. They remembered the rumors they heard that they just happened to pass on because the gossip was too good to pass up. I wonder if they ever threw stones at someone. I wonder if they thought of the misjudgments in their lives and the way they'd wrongly looked at others. I wonder if, in those moments...they wondered if their thoughts and actions had been justified. If they wished they could have taken what they had done and thought before they spoke, threw, or judged.

The major difference between the perceptive we have of Mary and the perceptive of the woman caught in adultery is simple: we don't judge Mary because we know something the people of her day didn't. We have received revelation only the Holy Spirit can give. Now we need to pray for the spiritual heart and perspective to rest in the grace of God for what we don't know and refuse to use what we do know against others.

Judgment is a dishonest place (Matthew 7:1-5). It is when we convince ourselves that we are above doing certain things because of a sense of self-esteem rather than divine mercy. We must avoid the temptation to cleverly analyze others and then tell them what we feel is wrong with them, all to avoid things we've done. We don't like to feel that helpless feeling, that total sense of void where nothing we say or does matters. We don't even feel like we can defend ourselves or speak up, no matter how we may feel about what we've done. Our lives and the lives of those we've known and judged flash before us. All we want is a little mercy...and in judgment, we don't find that.

Nobody wants to be the woman caught in adultery...but underneath it all, we are all her. Jesus stooped down and listed the sins of the leaders not to prove that they were no better than her, but to prove that they were her. There is a reason why she is unnamed: because she is all of us. We don't confide in others because we fear what they will say to us. We fear and avoid the stones of pity, criticism, loathing, envy, and hatred that people throw when they discover things about us. We don't trust other people because they are untrustworthy. We fear what they will say to other people. We fear that our honesty will cause them to never look at us the same way again, of the awkward strain and silences that result when we are honest with others. We fear that moment when we will be set in the city square because everyone will wind up knowing, as we lay buried under a pile of stones.

The Bible is full of open-ended situations where we don't

have the complete story. I believe God did this on purpose. We like to write in our own details, our own endings, write the story of the Bible from our own perspective. God doesn't give us the "why" because He wants us to outgrow our own temptations to project ourselves on the Word. In doing so, we learn about the power and grace of mercy over judgment. If we want to be effective witnesses of the Gospel, we need to make sure we aren't judging people in any form. We need to keep the stones on the ground and remember that moment when the Lord held her hand and said, "Neither do I condemn you." He was the only One there who had the right to condemn her, and He chose not to because He knew something everyone else didn't. We need to make the Lord Himself our model, knowing ourselves, knowing our lives, and knowing that it is only His mercy that grabs our hand and carries us to a better place.

In our lives, there will always be something we resisted that others did not, and something we didn't resist that someone else did. There will forever be situations we hear about where we think we would have done things differently, forgetting that we weren't in them and we probably don't know what we would do. All I can advise is think before you throw. Whoever, whatever...you will realize one day is you.

When we are called of God, everything God does within us is revolutionary and counterculture. That's not to say everything in our lives feels that way (obviously, we still have to do boring things like laundry and dishes), but that our greater purpose is different from the norm. While yes, He does call us to maintain a certain sense of decency and order to make sure that people aren't focused on our bad attitudes, undisciplined nature, or mere appearance, God always calls us to be different as people. We aren't here to do the general stuff that goes along with the status quo of society. Mary is no different in this statement. Mary was a challenge to every notion of her time, including the laws, rules, and regulations that existed to keep women in a specific place. While it was never Mary's intention to defy society to be "most blessed," she wasn't able to fall in line with everyone else and do what everyone else did.

Imagine being so young and faced with

engagement, marriage, and married life, all within a short enough window of time...and then, of all things, to have an angelic visit. This wasn't just your average, run-of-the-mill dream where an angel appears with a harp and invites you to sit on a cloud. Mary found out in her short angelic encounter that her entire life was going to change. Goodbye, ordinary life. Goodbye future. Goodbye normal. Hello revolutionary, different, and extraordinary. Mary was given a most awesome greeting – she was highly favored, and most blessed among all women – because she would give birth to a son, the Son of the Most High. She would call Him Jesus.

Notably perplexed and confused, Mary inquired as to how this was possible. She knew what pregnancy outside of marriage would mean for her: the end of her life in any semblance of normalcy. She wasn't so naive that she didn't know where babies came from. Knowing she hadn't done anything to have a baby, what gives, Angel Gabriel?

What a day that must have been.

Even with this startling news that must have caused Mary's entire life to flash before her eyes, she remained calm and inviting to the Spirit. With a level of quiet sanity I can't fathom, she reiterated that if this was God's will, then may it be done to her, as the messenger said. If this was the path God had for her, then she was going to walk it, knowing fully well what might result from it.

I respect Mary's restraint. I would have had dozens of questions and wanted to know more about this whole process. Mary, however, had enough faith to not know every detail of her future. In time, she would know all she needed to know. For now, it was time to handle other matters.

Joseph...being a man

We don't consider that for much of Mary's life, from this point forward, she experienced much of her personal life experience by herself. Yes, Joseph was there, but only to a certain extent. While many accounts try to depict

Joseph as benevolent and patient (which he might have been), it's more likely than not that he wasn't too impressed by the news of a virgin birth. We can sense this in his attitude, expressed in Scripture.

Matthew 1:18-25:

This is how the birth of Jesus the Messiah came about: His mother Mary was pledged to be married to Joseph, but before they came together, she was found to be pregnant through the Holy Spirit. Because Joseph her husband was faithful to the law, and yet did not want to expose her to public disgrace, he had in mind to divorce her quietly.

But after he had considered this, an angel of the Lord appeared to him in a dream and said, "Joseph, son of David, do not be afraid to take Mary home as your wife, because what is conceived in her is from the Holy Spirit. She will give birth to a son, and you are to give Him the Name Jesus, because He will save people from their sins."

All this took place to fulfill what the Lord had said through the prophet: "The virgin will conceive and give birth to a son, and they will call Him Immanuel" (which means, "God with us").

When Joseph woke up, he did what the angel of the Lord had commanded him and took Mary home as his wife. But he did not consummate their marriage until she gave birth to a son. And he gave Him the Name Jesus.

According to the Bible account, Mary and Joseph were in their betrothal period within a year leading up to their wedding. You would like to think that Joseph and Mary had some knowledge of each other, although it might have been on the limited side. Still, he most likely knew her enough to know her character, the kind of person she was, and he definitely knew her family to some degree. What do we see here? Joseph intended to divorce Mary because she was found to be pregnant and they were still in that window of time where he was free to divorce her and find someone else.

Why did he intend to divorce her? Because Joseph suspected she'd been unfaithful to him. He was concerned about his bloodline and reputation. He disliked the idea of raising a child that wasn't his. The passage tells us he was faithful to the law – in other words, he was devoted to live by the law to its fullest extent. According to the law, he had the right to a divorce, so he planned to divorce Mary and get it over with quickly and quietly. He didn't want to expose her to open disgrace, but at the same time, he didn't want to risk his life and future, either. In essence, he was prepared to bow to cultural opinion and dump a pregnant woman on the street to avoid public question.

Nice guy, huh? We see all the sweet pictures of "the holy family," as we call them on Christmas cards, but the reality of their lives was probably far different than our fantasies. We obviously don't consider their day in and day out, what it was like to be a couple with this unique challenge in their day and age. Even though Joseph was responsive to Mary's situation, that response only came about because of God's prompting. By the standards of her day, Mary was another unwed, pregnant teenager. When people saw her on the street, they turned their heads and looked the other way. They gossiped about her and made judgments when no one was looking. If they did this to her, even though God moved Joseph to remain with her, it means that Joseph lived with their taunts and judgments as well, also suspecting Mary was unfaithful to him. Even though Joseph did accept the circumstances, we must remember Joseph was still a human being. He lived with a woman who had a child that was not his biological son. Son of God or not, given the time frame in which they lived, the emphasis on paternity (particularly firstborn sons), and the strict cultural mores, I am sure there were many situations where difficulty, disagreement, and alienation arose. Mary faced much of what she experienced alone, probably afraid to share her fears and concerns with Joseph, learning to rely on God and the sense of assurance He gave to her as she walked out this most difficult task with her own life.

It's also important to realize that Mary's acceptance of God's will in her life could have most definitely gotten her killed. According to the letter of the law (which nobody really understood or applied properly in her time), Mary was branded an adulterer. By the law that Joseph held dear, she should have been stoned for her pregnancy. Then add the fact that it was a virgin birth – a yeah right, get real, tell me something else absurd – moment. All the while, Mary was calm. She was going to have the Son of God, a holy child, unlike any other.

What do we learn? Nothing is impossible with God!

Insignificant significance

There are numerous writings which surfaced in the early centuries of Christianity that attempt to make Mary divine. Rumors exploded and continue to circulate that she was conceived without sin, a goddess, lived a sinless life, and so on and so forth. Even believers back then had a hard time fathoming a woman could carry Immanuel, God With Us, and just be an everyday, ordinary human being. Yet what these rumors truly do is deter from the fact that Mary's life was significant because it was insignificant to everyone but God. God knew that Mary mattered and her choices mattered. While to the world Mary might have been a nobody and a nothing from nowhere, Mary mattered to God and Mary proves that when God gets ahold of us (and we get ahold of God), God turns our ordinary into extraordinary.

Luke 1:26-38:

In the sixth month of Elizabeth's pregnancy, God sent the angel Gabriel to Nazareth, a town in Galilee, to a virgin pledged to be married to a man named Joseph, a descendant of David. The virgin's name was Mary. The angel went to her and said, "Greetings, you who are highly favored! The Lord is with you."

Mary was greatly troubled at his words and wondered what kind of greeting this might be. But the angel said to her, "Do not be afraid, Mary; you have found favor with God. You will conceive and give birth to a Son, and you are to call Him Jesus. He will be great and will be called the Son of the Most High. The Lord God will give Him the throne of His father David, and He will reign over Jacob's descendants forever; His Kingdom will never end."

"How will this be," Mary asked the angel, "since I am a virgin?"

The angel answered, the Holy Spirit will come on you, and the power of the Most High will overshadow you. So the Holy One to be born will be called the Son of God. Even Elizabeth your relative is going to have a child in her old age, and she who was said to be unable to conceive is in her sixth month. For no word from God will ever fail."

"I am the Lord's servant," Mary answered. "May your word to me be fulfilled." Then the angel left her.

This fact alone should give us all great hope. If Mary started her own life as a "nobody" in the eyes of the world and God used her to change history, then God can use you and me, too. That is our hope. It's not about where we come from, being famous, or coming from the right family. It's saying "yes" at the right moment and then following through on it. As your life changes, other lives are changed because of your "yes" to God!

A virgin birth was possible for God because Mary was willing to be used by God. Using this example, it's possible for God to do anything through and within us that He desires, if we are willing to say "yes" to His plan. God needed Mary's "yes" to complete His plan, and we must consider that Mary had the right to say "no" at any time. Still, faced with these odds, she didn't say no. That needs to be acknowledged as a part of the plan. Her yes gave her eternal significance, one we are still talking about today, right down to our present age.

This means: No matter how unimportant you may feel or how irrelevant your voice may seem to the world, what you have to offer is a part of the plan. What you have to offer is that important. If God With Us can be born of a woman, God can pick you up and change your life and the life of the entire world through you. God can give you victory over your enemies. He can give you insight to get out of your difficult circumstance. To get there, we must first say "yes" to God's plan, which may involve things we don't always like.

I am sure Mary didn't enjoy the barrage of questions about her reputation and the judgment she faced from others. Mary went from being a quiet nobody and nothing to being the talk of everyone's town, the story on everyone's lips. (If you are praying to be famous, think about this experience: a lot goes along with it that isn't pleasant, and we never consider.) She knew exactly what they were thinking, without any of them having to say a word. Then after she had Jesus, she had to deal with the fact that Jesus didn't belong to her and she would have to give Him to the One from which He came.

Paying the price to be different

The things we have discussed about Mary's experience should already have us thinking. Every one of us has stereotyped Mary, Joseph, even Jesus in some ways that are not realistic. We tend to gloss over Biblical characters, making their lives and experiences deeply out of touch with who they were and the realities of everyday life. We think Mary's proclamation of being "most blessed meant she had no problems and waltzed through life, without difficulty or feelings.

Mary was "most blessed" because she paid a price that someone else was unwilling to pay. People who are blessed, happy and fortunate to be envied do different things than the mainline experience. They make a stand against the world to be different. They allow themselves to be a people who are transformed, changed, and different, ready to work and do what God would have them to do. Of course, there is a slight catch involved here, one that we don't hear many people talk about.

If we want to be blessed, we must walk away from things that aren't the answer for us in life. Something that might be just fine for someone else might not work out that way for you, and if you try to do it, you might face a disaster. Being most blessed means turning off the blinders that cause us to look at everyone but God, those that cause us to compare ourselves to others, and open ourselves up to something else, something greater that God has for us.

Saying yes to God means pursuing things through that others don't and following through on every dimension of God's plan, in detail. We don't just walk God's plan; we live it, intimately, up close and personal. It's not always comfortable, nor do we always want to follow through on every detail. Sometimes we expect to take one path, and wind up taking another, only to find ourselves exactly where God would want us to be from the beginning. God divinely orchestrates the general course of our lives but allows us the freedom to make our choices. The more we follow His will, the more we understand Him better, and we come to love Him in a deeper way.

We can't get there, however, if we are obsessed with what everyone else is doing and what everything they do looks or sounds like. What you go through is going to look different than what someone else goes through. God might ask you to break all the rules through your own life and experience, just like He asked of Mary. That means you will be misunderstood, misjudged, left out, and set apart. Not everyone can handle it. It means life, as you know it ends, and something new begins.

A baby shower to remember

If you've ever been to a baby shower or had one yourself, what did you do at it? Most baby showers are full of corny games, gifts for mom and baby, cake, and camaraderie as a woman prepares to become a mother. Some people love baby showers, and some can't stand them, but they are often an important step in a pregnant woman's experience.

Elizabeth and Mary had a different sort of baby shower, if you will. There were no guests except for themselves and the Holy Spirit. There were no gifts, save the spiritual indwelling of the Spirit. And rather than play games, these two women spoke of the joy of their pregnancies by heralding the coming day when every earthly empire would be overthrown by their God. Their pregnancies weren't about male heirs and property transfers down generations. In a time and place that had no use for Elizabeth's aging pregnancy nor Mary's unwed teenage promise, the two lived their realities as the only people who recognized the powerful prophecies they carried.

Imagine being the only two people in the world who know the overthrow of everything is to come...and that you're part of it because you're pregnant with the revolutionaries who shall both herald and lead this process. There's responsibility ahead, promises to keep, and the need for these two unsuspecting women to stand as radicals themselves. Surely, not meek and mild, but bold and empowered for the road ahead.

I've heard contrasting speculation as to why Mary visited Elizabeth, especially why she stayed for such a long time. We know Elizabeth was Mary's cousin, thus making John the Baptist and Jesus second cousins. Elizabeth was old and on in years, and Mary was pregnant with Jesus. She most likely made this visit, not as a mere social call, but to preserve and help save her life. Getting her away from her hometown was the first step to preserving life in a culture that was all-too-eager to have a big, old-fashioned stoning at her expense.

Regardless of the reason why Mary visited Elizabeth, the meeting of these two women was very important in terms of their lives and their blessings.

Luke 1:39-56:

Soon afterward, Mary hurried to a city in the mountain region of Judah. She entered Zechariah's home and greeted Elizabeth.

When Elizabeth heard the greeting, she felt the baby kick. Elizabeth was filled with the Holy Spirit. She said in a loud voice, "You are the most blessed of all women, and blessed is the child that you will have. I feel blessed that the mother of my Lord is visiting me. As soon as I heard your greeting, I felt the baby jump for joy. You are blessed for believing that the Lord would keep His promise to you."

Mary said,

"My soul praises the Lord's greatness!
My spirit finds its joy in God, my Savior,
 because He has looked favorably on me, His humble
 servant.

"From now on, all people will call me blessed
  because the Almighty has done great things to me.
    His Name is holy.
      For those who fear Him,
        His mercy lasts throughout every generation.

"He displayed His mighty power.
  He scattered those who think too highly of themselves.
    He pulled strong rulers from their thrones.
      He honored humble people.
        He fed hungry people with good food.
          He sent rich people away with nothing.

"He remembered to help His servant Israel forever.
  This is the promise He made to our ancestors,
    to Abraham and his descendants."

Mary stayed with Elizabeth about three months and then went back home. (GW)

The first two people in the New Testament reported to be filled with the Holy Spirit were Mary (to become pregnant with Jesus) and secondly, now, Elizabeth. When she was filled with the Holy Spirit, she spoke out loudly, about the blessing that Mary had received among all women. In being filled with the Spirit, Elizabeth proclaimed what was already true — that she was blessed, and so was her baby to come. Jesus wasn't born yet and yes, there was promise of the child who too would be blessed. Mary and Jesus were individually blessed here — Mary was blessed among all women, and then Jesus was also blessed, showing us the divine blessing that was not just in Jesus, but was Jesus Himself. This was no ordinary child; He was a blessing to the entire world, and to us, right down, to today.

Yet there is still Mary's blessing, which not many dare to write about in modern times. I think we are afraid it will take focus off Jesus. If anything, it reaffirms His relevance while celebrating the commitment Mary made to be His mother.

Mary made the choice to bear the Son of God. All by itself, that is a feat that made her blessed among all women — but she was also blessed for her belief. Mary's life and her testimony proved that she did believe all things were possible with God. Even Mary herself can't keep quiet at her gathering with Elizabeth, because the details of it are so incredibly blessed. Mary saw into the future as well as her own reality and was able to see that God intends good for His people. He sends good things to all of us, each at its own appointed time.

The "yes" heard round the world

We know that Jesus is our Savior, but do we realize that Jesus changed the whole world? Jesus left a mark on history as well as spirituality. Every religious system known to humanity made room for His singular life, and many can't even really account for why it was done. They may not acknowledge the fullness of Who He is, but they couldn't ignore Him, either. The life of Jesus and His purpose in this earth was not a little thing.

This means that what Mary did was beyond important. In her own right, she played a role in salvation history. She was not the Savior, but the one who allowed God to work in her so the Savior could come into the world. She had to make a sacrifice of herself so that could happen, and it made a difference in the lives of every person the world over.

Luke 2:7-19:

She gave birth to her firstborn Son. She wrapped Him in strips of cloth and laid Him in a manger because there wasn't any room for them in the inn.

Shepherds were in the fields near Bethlehem. They were taking turns watching their flock during the night. An angel from the Lord suddenly appeared to them. The glory of the Lord filled the area with light, and they were terrified. The angel said to them, "Don't be afraid! I have good news for you, a message that will fill everyone with joy. Today your Savior, Christ the Lord, was born in David's city. This is how you will recognize Him: You will find an infant wrapped in strips of cloth and lying in a manger."

Suddenly, a large army of angels appeared with the angel. They were praising God by saying,

"Glory to God in the highest heaven,
    and on earth peace to those who have His good will!"

The angels left them and went back to heaven. The shepherds said to each other, "Let's go to Bethlehem and see what the Lord has told us about."

They went quickly and found Mary and Joseph with the baby, Who was lying in a manger. When they saw the child, they repeated what they had been told about Him. Everyone who heard the shepherds' story was amazed.

Mary treasured all these things in her heart and always thought about them. (GW)

The Bible tells us Mary treasured these early experiences in her heart and pondered, as she wondered about what was to come. She recalled her prophetic words, those that connected Her Son's existence with the overthrow of earthly oppression. She thought about the things within her, those moments that would come that nobody could identify with. She pondered her upcoming challenges. She thought about the things that even Joseph didn't know and wouldn't understand. They were the things she had to take to God directly and realize He was the One Who would understand, because He was the One Who asked her to do this. He knew she could handle what was to come, because it was His Son, that part of Himself, that they took, too. She knew Who her Son was, and it was all that much harder to walk that walk and not be able to share it with anyone but God.

Mary reminds us that if we say "yes" and it has a big impact, we will experience some things that others won't experience because they haven't been through them. I can testify as an apostle of God that there are a lot of things I have gone through in this walk that I know nobody this side of heaven could have ever imagined. It wasn't their experience to have. It wasn't their walk, it wasn't their call, and it wasn't what they said "yes" to do. I said "yes" to it, but I still wanted to know why others didn't understand or seem to be able to help me through it. They didn't because they couldn't. It wasn't for them to know, or understand, or recognize. It was my walk, my vow, and my life.

I needed to stop looking for people to sympathize with the issues I had and develop a deeper relationship with God instead. I am the first one to agree and believe that, as a rule, many believers are disconnected from one another and that it's important for us to reach out and support each other in our trials. At the same time, it is unrealistic for us to believe the support of others will change our situations or make the calling we have different than it is. We learn how to handle the calling God has given us through God and the wise leadership appointed in our lives. By following His direction, we accept and learn to manage it. No matter how many people sit with us, hold our hands, pray with us or for us, or talk us through, the way we get through what we must go through is by God's direction.

Along with this, we can see the deep intimacy Mary experienced with God. Part of being most blessed means we find something special in our relationship with God. In it, God gives us something others can't give to us. Doing important things means that sometimes we stand by ourselves, with our own griefs, sorrows, questions, and feelings. Through it all, we trust that God will reveal Himself to us as a powerful comforting Father Who knows just why He calls us, and just what we can handle.

A revolutionary at heart

I Samuel 10:6-7:

The Spirit of the LORD will come powerfully upon you, and you will prophesy with them; and you will be changed into a different person. Once these signs are fulfilled, do whatever your hand finds to do, for God is with you.

We like to talk about change and change coming our way. It heralds sermons, words spoken in prayer lines, and prayer requests. We hope for it, long for it, and believe for it, often in unspecific terms. However, the truth is that change is hard. It's hard to be the first one that we know, the first one in our circles, or maybe even the first one in history to do something that goes against societal norms. Being different means defying convention, family traditions, and finding new connections and paths to complete His will. Every single one of us needs to ask ourselves, do we have what it takes to be Mary in our modern world?

God isn't going to ask us to be a part of a virgin birth. That was a done deal, something that happened one time and is now over. God will ask us, though, to birth things that the world deems impossible. He will call us to do things others say we can't do or won't work out. He will ask us to believe in Him because He believes in our abilities, as He works within us. We might have to walk alone and do things that are hard or undesirable, things that will cause risk to our stellar reputations and change how others view us. We have to be willing to put life and liberty and everything we think we have on the line to do the will of God and change history through our yes for Him.

Many say yes with their mouths to look good in front of everyone, with their plans and super-spiritual sounding ideas. Truth be told, they often back off quickly when God asks them to do something they don't want to do. Above all things, being a revolutionary for God and having that revolutionary spirit at heart means we are willing to be obedient and walk out that obedience in our lives. We receive God's abundant, radical, biggest blessing as we walk out the walk, not just because we make an agreement to do something that sounds good to us at the time. Mary probably second-guessed her decision at times, but she never reneged when it got difficult. She kept walking forward, through it, and on to whatever stop was next in her life.

Bottom line of what Mary teaches us? We can't be blessed if we don't obey.

Reflections

- What is holding you back from receiving God's blessing in your life?

- What aspects of your life and call do you need to examine and develop with God, versus other people?

- How can you relate to Mary's story and experience?

CHAPTER THREE

Jael

- Warring Women Win! -

*FIGHT THE GOOD FIGHT OF THE FAITH. TAKE HOLD OF THE ETERNAL LIFE
TO WHICH YOU WERE CALLED WHEN YOU MADE YOUR GOOD CONFESSION
IN THE PRESENCE OF MANY WITNESSES.*
(I TIMOTHY 6:12)

WOMEN in the military is a big, huge deal in the western world. Over here, we debate whether women should be in combat, on the front lines, or in specific positions of military authority. In other countries, such is not so. Military service is often compulsory for all sexes within a certain age span. Some require a designated commitment of at least two or three years, to be completed before someone turns a certain age. This is not true in western culture, because we have spent generations and generations treating women as if they are going to break. We have grown up with the concept that women aren't aggressive, never get angry, can't fight back in trying situations, and that women are helpless and in need of men to rescue and take care of them. If we listen to society, it sounds like women are weak, silly, and incompetent, incapable of things as serious as military discipline and battle.

Many of these ideas are now found in church and

promoted as Biblical ideals. We hear it whenever we are told that women shouldn't be in the military or in combat, or that they are weak and incapable of living their lives without a man to lead them. Those who promote these ideals trip up when it comes to discussing Deborah, the military leader of Israel early in the book of Judges. More of them don't even have words for the woman we are going to look at here, whose name is Jael. In all my years in church, I have heard only one message on Jael from the pulpit, and that message was preached by a spiritual daughter of mine at a women's conference hosted by our ministry.

Jael was a woman no one would suspect had a warrior within her, waiting to come out. In fact, nothing about Jael's conduct within the confines of our story was remotely "ladylike," poised, weak, helpless, or incompetent. She didn't wait for someone else to do the job because she was ready and prepared to become "most blessed" for her actions which secured the victory in battle.

Jael is here for every little girl who never measured up to society's ideals for being ladylike, and who now lead the way for something more important than whether her napkin is folded properly. She gives us all permission to be the woman that God has created us to be, that it's all right to be tough, it's all right to be different, and that there is no right or wrong way to be a woman. Important? Timely? Most definitely. Universally accepted? Probably not.

Like Jael or not, here she comes.

Women in the time of Jael

Numbers 24:21:

Then he saw the Kenites and delivered this message: "You have a permanent place to live. Your nest is built in a rock." (GW)

Judges 4:11:

Heber the Kenite had separated from the other Kenites (the descendants of Hobab, Moses' father-in-law). Heber went as far away as the oak tree at Zaanannim near Kedesh and set up his tent. (GW)

We know very little of Jael's life beyond the Bible telling us she was the wife of Heber the Kenite. The Kenites were an ancient nomadic clan who were not Hebrews, but often worked closely with them and were interconnected with ancient Israeli culture. That's about all we have of Jael's history. We can see she lived at the same time as Deborah, but we don't know who was older, younger, or if they knew one another before the time in Judges when both women came into focus.

It's unfortunate that we don't really know what period in history the book of Judges specifically covers. There's speculation over the expanse of time it might cover, and there's no consensus. That means we don't know when Deborah or Jael lived. We can gather from their story that female leadership and women in military service was not unheard of, although it might not have been as common as male leadership and military service. These facts are supported in different ancient historical periods and lend credibility to the fact that societies didn't always treat, nor regard, women in quite the same way they have in more recent history. Things weren't always like they are now, and that should make us more aware that the battles we fight as pertain to female military involvement and position are based on more recent traditions rather than actual eternal truths.

Women in Deborah and Jael's time most likely experienced arranged marriage, including dowries and bridal prices, and probably had little to do with their marital choices or options. Women also probably did not enjoy equal status within society, considering that rulers always have a certain level of privilege that non-rulers do not enjoy. Overall, however, Deborah and Jael challenge a lot of notions, societal customs, and ideas that we often take as Gospel...which clearly are not.

Deborah, mother of Israel

I can't rightly talk about Jael without talking some about Deborah. Deborah's battle, as Israel's military leader, found victory thanks to Jael.

Judges 4:1-5:

Again the Israelites did evil in the eyes of the LORD, now that Ehud was dead. So the LORD sold them into the hands of Jabin king of Canaan, who reigned in Hazor. Sisera, the commander of his army, was based in Harosheth Haggoyim. Because he had nine hundred chariots fitted with iron and had cruelly oppressed the Israelites for twenty years, they cried to the LORD for help.

Deborah, a prophetess, the wife of Lappidoth, was leading Israel at that time. She held court under the Palm of Deborah between Ramah and Bethel in the hill country of Ephraim, and the Israelites went up to her to have their disputes decided.

The entire book of Judges is, of sorts, a lesson in anarchy. The nation of Israel went from ruler to ruler, individuals who intervened to deliver the nation when its punishments for idolatry became burdensome. Deborah enters the picture when Israel was in a state of chaos. They'd done evil, acted in disobedience, and lived under an oppressive ruler for twenty years. As a result, the nation fell into disarray. There were no roads, government, and the nation did not function as a cohesive group.

Sounds like the ideal time for two women to walk in and clean up the mess. These two women, Deborah and Jael, literally became the mothers of that nation.

Deborah was a prophetess, but she did not just exercise spiritual authority. She was also a judge, which means she was in a governmental position, responsible for the day-to-day leadership of Israel. The Bible tells us she would dwell under a palm tree and people would come to her with their various disputes. If someone had a question about property, legal discussions, legislation, or disputes between people, she was the person to see. As a prophetess, her spiritual authority and insights gave her the ability to lead people wisely and with guidance. Here she was, responsible for leading this entire nation!

We learn that Deborah was the wife of Lappidoth...and we don't learn another thing about him or their situation. We don't know about his job, how he felt about Deborah's position, or what his feelings were about his life. Lappidoth's position was to support Deborah, not be a nag and complain that his needs weren't getting met. In the synergy the two of them had, Lappidoth knew what being married to Deborah meant, and he took responsibility where it was needed. (Let that be a lesson to all the men out there who have a wife with a calling that demands her time and attention!)

As a side note, I think we need to consider this, especially if we are in positions of church or secular leadership. We hear so much that tears us down and makes it sound like we, as women, should feel guilty for pursuing things that God has called us to do or things that interest us. We feel guilty when we go home, like we are taking time away from those who are closest to us. This often makes us feel like we don't do things right. Deborah couldn't run around with a long and complicated guilt complex and successfully run Israel. She had to establish some limits and boundaries, and she and her husband had to work out what was best for them, not what someone else told them was best for them.

When we are called to do things for God, we have a different set of priorities from other people. This isn't to say we shirk responsibility, but it is to say that Lappidoth proves we don't attend to spiritual things without the help of others. Woman of God, stop trying to do too much and stop feeling so guilty. If you truly believe your spouse is heaven-sent, then you should find they recognize what God has called you to do and ways to be supportive of that. It shouldn't be one-sided or so complicated, as it too often is. There should be no guilt trips and no bottom lines, only negotiations and support. How couples work out their divisions of labor and home support is up to them, not to the impossible notions we attach to them.

We go on to see in Judges that God gave the Israelites a specific command: go and take back their nation from their captors. Even though God did place the enemies in the hands of the Israelites, God still expected them to take those captors. He didn't just erase them off the planet and make them magically disappear. If the army was faithful to God's instructions, they would gain victory over their enemy captors, because that was God's promise to them.

The Israelites were expected to embrace and trust in that promise. This involved stepping out in faith and no matter how much they might have been afraid, uncomfortable, or uncertain in how it would all go down, they were expected to trust that promise and obey their God.

The victory goes to a woman

Judges 4:6-24:

She sent for Barak son of Abinoam from Kedesh in Naphtali and said to him, "The LORD, the God of Israel, commands you: 'Go, take with you ten thousand men of Naphtali and Zebulun and lead them up to Mount Tabor. I will lead Sisera, the commander of Jabin's army, with his chariots and his troops to the Kishon River and give him into your hands.'"

Barak said to her, "If you go with me, I will go; but if you don't go with me, I won't go."

"Certainly I will go with you," said Deborah. But because of the course you are taking, the honor will not be yours, for the LORD will deliver Sisera into the hands of a woman." So Deborah went with Barak to Kedesh. There barak Zebulun and Naphtali, and ten thousand men went up under his command. Deborah also went with him.

Now Heber the Kenite had left the other Kenites, the descendants of Hobab, Moses' brother-in-law, and pitch ed his tent by the great tere in Zaanannim near Kedesh.

When they told Sisera that Barak son of Abinosam had gone up to Mount Tabor, Sisera summoned from Harosheth Haggoyim to the Kishon River all his men and his nine hundred chariots fitted with iron.

Then Deborah said to Barak, "Go! This is the day the LORD has given Sisera into your hands. Has not the LORD gone ahead of you?" So Barak went down Mount Tabor, with ten thousand men following him. At Barak's advance, the LORD routed Sisera and all his chariots and army by the sword, and Sisera got down from his chariot and fled on foot.

Barak pursued the chariots and army as far as Harosheth Haggoyim, and all Sisera's troops fell by the sword; not a man was left. Sisera, meanwhile, fled on foot to the tent of Jael, the wife of Heber the Kenite, because there was an alliance between Jabin king of Hazor and the family of Heber the Kenite.

Jael went out to meet Sisera and said to him, "Come, my lord, come right in. Don't be afraid." So he entered her tent, and she covered him with a blanket.

"I'm thirsty," he said. "Please give me some water." She opened a skin of milk, gave him a drink, and covered him up.

"Stand in the doorway of the tent," he told her, "If someone comes by and asks you, 'Is anyone here?' say 'No.'"

But Jael, Heber's wife, picked up a tent peg and a hammer and went quietly to him while he lay fast asleep, exhausted. She drove the peg through his temple into the ground, and he died.

BLESSED THOUGHTS:

I am a warring woman

I have a sword by my side
And a peg behind my back;
I am ready and able
To fight the enemy's attack.

I am a woman...
A warring woman...
And I win.

My life flashes clear before my eyes.
There is nothing you can throw at me
That will take me by surprise;
I am thoroughly prepared for the task ahead:

I am a woman...
A warring woman...
And I win.

The Devil's been at me from day one
But I never back down...
There is too much work to be done:
In this battle for life, truth, and love.

I am a woman...
A warring woman...
And I win.

It's not easy to be a woman today.
Everyone shouts and screams,
Telling me to do it their way;
But I refuse to back down, or to play their game.

I am a woman...
A warring woman...
And I win.

They tell me to marry, to have children, to be
Everything within the "American dream"
But what they do not know and cannot see

Is God has called me to be who He has for me to be!

I am a woman...
A warring woman...
And I win.

I can be charming and quiet,
But don't take surprise;
I am feisty, fiery, and lively;
There is fire behind these eyes.
I am ready to fight at the sound of His call:

I am a woman...
A warring woman...
And I win.

I've lived through the fire, the torment, the flood;
I've seen abuse and mistreatment
But I stand because of His Blood...
And I refuse to be a victim, I am a victor because:

I am a woman...
A warring woman...
And I win.

So don't think you'll kill me, no stronger I'll be
And the battle rages on,
And I stand firmer within me;
And the battle tarries long, as the Lord calls me to go...

Because I am a woman...
A warring woman...
And I win.

Barak came by in pursuit of Sisera, and Jael went out to meet him. "Come," she said, "I will show you the man you're looking for." So he went in with her, and there lay Sisera with the tent peg through his temple – dead.

On that day God subdued Jabin, king of Canaan before the Israelites. And the hand of the Israelites pressed harder and harder against Jabin king of Canaan until they destroyed him.

Barak, a military general, seeks Deborah – a woman, the prophetess and leader of his country – requesting her to accompany him on this military journey to conquer their captors. Now let me say this, I don't believe Barak was weak, or not tough enough as a man, or any of that nonsense we often hear spread around by people who are threatened at the idea of a woman in leadership or a man coming to a female leader and requesting her presence. 10,000 men followed the command of Deborah (and we still hear about men giving women a hard time for being in the military!). I believe Barak knew the relevance of this battle, and he desired to have Deborah present because she had the needed spiritual insight to bring about military victory. Barak's obedience to his leader meant the victory would not go to him, but to a woman. This was God's plan. In a bigger sense, this was the intentional way God planned for victory to favor the Israelites. Nobody would see it coming! As Barak recognized order, he knew and would recognize God's plan for this situation involved the tactics of a woman.

Think about that, for a few moments. The hand of victory would not go to a man, but to a woman. The world in which Jael and Deborah lived was not one of promised victory for women. This makes it most significant that the fate of an entire nation rested in the powerful skill of this one woman, Jael. It was a victory not just for Israel, but for all women who didn't have identities and still had a societal "place."

It's even more relevant that this victory went to a woman who, most likely, wasn't even an Israelite! Her husband, Heber the Kenite, was friends with the Canaanite king! That's why Sisera went to visit her tent in the first place. Without foreknowledge that Sisera would come, Jael's husband rose to occasion and called everyone he knew to fight on Israel's side, believing their cause was right. It's interesting to see how both Deborah and Lappidoth and now Jael and Heber clearly worked as part of the same team. There wasn't the sting of competition we often see in relationships, and that was how they won the victory. When strife is present, nothing gets done. When teamwork is present, all things get done.

As the army advanced, now with Heber's men and their support, Sisera's army fell in its entirety that day, with not a man left standing. Sisera himself, however, got away.

Where did Sisera go? Right to the tent of Jael, wife of Heber the Kenite! Funny how he wound up thinking he could find allies there and, instead, found himself right in the entrapment of his enemy.

Jael wasn't a woman we would think of as a great warrior or even one who would be "most blessed." She wasn't powerful or wealthy. She didn't have a political position. She probably wasn't someone regarded as "important" in society. But within Jael was the heart of a warrior. She was not a woman of fear; she was strong and bold. She was not weak, and this enemy would not get past her. She wasn't afraid to do what needed to be done, and she knew what needed to be done when it needed doing. She didn't even worry about her reputation – she didn't step back and think twice, but she just acted as was needed.

Jael used what she had to entrap the enemy. She was not a woman who was going to be victimized, but she used what she had – her charm – to ensnare him. Being a man who was weakened by battle, he walked right into her trap. He accepted her hospitality and walked right into the tent. Looking at Jael through the eyes of cultural stereotypes, Sisera saw Jael only as hospitable, feminine, and offering her wiles for his cares (who says cooking and hospitality can't be dangerous!). Keeping this in mind, who knows, had she not acted quickly, what might have happened to her. She was on a mission from God, and we have no indication she was afraid. She wasn't afraid to be alone with this man, or that he might make a move on her, because Jael knew God was with her and what she was doing was God-ordained as she moved on instinct.

Jael knew how to play the feminine card: she covered up Sisera and provided him drink and comfort. He never suspected a thing, and he allowed himself to be set up for the kill. When it was time to stand and make her move, she did. Instead of standing watch as Sisera asked, she drove a tent peg into his head...and that was the end of Sisera. Jael was able to present the enemy to Barak, dead and defeated. As promised, God gave the victory to a woman, Jael!

Women can be blessed in battle

One of the reasons we don't hear about Deborah and Jael much is because it seems, at least on the surface, they represent a violent nature we believe contrary to femininity. When we talk about spiritual battle, we don't tend to think of women as aggressive or victorious in spiritual warfare against the enemy. It's never a topic for a women's conference and is never something we consider when we hear the verses stated in service. Even if we go outside of our immediate Christian circles into some pagan groups that are supposedly all about women, they don't always embrace the side of a woman that is a warrior. Women who are warlike or battlers are regarded as "vengeful," and such behavior is always stereotyped in a certain way: and as being wrong.

The notion that women can't be warriors – whether in the natural or in the spiritual – is just as much a sexist commentary as it is to say women should stay at home and have no lives or interests outside of their homes and families. This often manifests in a very contradictory message given to women: they should be strong in the Spirit, but God wants them to live and be totally passive as people.

Matthew 11:11-15:

Truly I tell you, among those born of women there has not risen anyone greater than John the Baptist; yet whoever is least in the Kingdom of heaven is greater than he. From the days of John the Baptist until now, the Kingdom of heaven has been subjected to violence, and violent people have been raiding it. For all the Prophets and the Law prophesied until John. And if you are willing to accept it, he is the Elijah who was to come. Whoever has ears, let them hear.

Deborah and Jael break stereotypes that many don't want to admit are just that – stereotypes. They prove women can still be women: beautiful, powerful, and still do what needs to be done in battle when the time comes to do it. They also prove women are key to spiritual battles and very key to victory in our lives. How do we do this? How do we find the blessing in the battle?

The key to stepping up is being aggressive in our pursuit of victory. Jael knew the balance between being a woman and a woman of God and knew how to use both for the advantage of the battle. Just because we are women who become women of God doesn't mean we cease being women. It also doesn't mean we have to walk around like we are in mourning all the time. Life is to be lived, and spiritual warfare reminds us of the need to live it, and do so with intense pursuit.

Another very vital thing we must recognize is that Jael and Deborah were not people who were walking around in vindictiveness. Jael didn't have a bone to pick with every man who rejected her. Deborah wasn't in a permanent state of fury and anger. Sisera wasn't Jael's ex-boyfriend who left her for another girl and now she was ready to get back at him. He didn't run into her car or steal from her house. Their motives weren't fueled by endless relationship drama. To define the actions of Jael or Deborah as vindictive is incorrect. They were not blinded by emotions or trying to make up for something or get back at someone for something. They were in a very real battle, acting strategically to win that battle.

These two Biblical women show us the difference between vindictiveness and aggression, and it's an important polarity. We all know women (and all people alike, not letting anyone out of this one) can be particularly vindictive. We become vindictive when we are made to be victims. When we are victimized in some way, we naturally become angry. Vindictiveness causes us to seek revenge. But if we walk in necessary aggression dependent on situation, we aren't vindictive. By doing so, we stand against a world that desires to victimize us. While aggression is an active expression, vindictiveness is always a hindsight reaction to something else. It never contributes to productivity. It might make someone feel good in the moment, but in the long run, it doesn't accomplish much.

Deborah and Jael were aggressive in these situations because such aggression was justified. This means we need to assess our own levels of aggression and anger in our lives, especially to make sure we pursue the correct enemy at the right time. It is unbecoming for anyone (as in all of humanity) to pursue displaced hostility or aggression. Healing is needed to make sure we pursue the battle we are in currently, not things from an earlier point in time that are still bothering us. Living in embitterment isn't blessed and blocks us from receiving the blessings God wishes to bestow upon us.

In the reverse, however, there are plenty of women who are afraid of being aggressive and moving forward with what God has for them because they consider such a pursuit to be wrong or unseemly for a woman. If you want to win the battle, you need to aggressively pursue what God has for you and make sure that the enemy does not get the victory in your life.

Jael was also a woman who would not be a victim. The world encourages us to be victims; it gives us the message it's wrong to fight back or for a cause, and that whatever happens to us is our fault. Jael proves such is a lie, and we need to pick up a little of Jael in our lives as we put down the fear we often experience and feel about life in general. We need to emulate this within ourselves, because we can't be afraid to fight back when things come against us or try to attack us.

Many of us have been victimized at some point in our lives. We need to know what happened to us was not our fault. We have done (and continue to do) the best we know, processing the massive guilt, fear, and intimidation that was thrust upon us by our perpetrators. This doesn't make us bad, weak, or wrong. It means someone else used force and intimidation to harm us and make us believe something was our fault, when it wasn't. For any woman who has been through this, it is time to stand up like Jael and get in touch with your inner warrior. It doesn't mean you have to go and hunt down whoever hurt you, but it does mean you need to stand up and fight to have your victory...because you are worth it. At some point in time, it's time to fight back, because you need to fight for your life.

Jeremiah 31:22:

How long wilt thou go about, O thou backsliding daughter? for the LORD hath created a new thing in the earth, A woman shall compass a man. (KJV)

The women of God have always been aggressive in one way or another because their stands make them notable for the Kingdom. Women who are permanently weak or passive are not usable by God, because they are too easily distracted or frightened to stand where God wants them to be. A woman who knows when it's time to be aggressive is focused on her goal and how to get there.

It is so vital we are strong and forceful in the things that merit our force. We can't sit idly by and expect the Kingdom to come along with and to us. Yes, salvation is free, but we must also recognize the importance in working with God to bring about good results as we actively pursue life. We must resolve to not be captive anymore, not be victims anymore, and be overcomers against every enemy, no matter how big, scary, or intimidating they may be.

We need to be the woman that they come to and say, "If you come with us, we will go with you." We need to be the ones that they seek out as leaders or trusted and respected women, because they recognize the strength we have inside and that it is needed for that situation. We also need to be the women who have celebrated victories and stands, who aren't surrounded by people who constantly criticize us and make us feel bad because what we have done is different. We need to be led by God, not constantly led by the thoughts and opinions of other people.

Warring women win!

Judges 5: 1 -7:

On that day Deborah and Barak son of Abinoam sang
this song:

"When the princes in Israel take the lead,
  when the people willingly offer themselves −
  praise the LORD!
"Hear this, you kings! Listen, you rulers!
I, even I, will sing to the LORD;
  I will praise the LORD, the God of Israel, in song.

"O LORD, when You went out from Seir,
  when You marched from the land of Edom,
  the earth shook, the heavens poured,
  the clouds poured down water.
  The mountains quaked before the LORD, the
    One of Sinai,
  before the LORD, the God of Israel.

"In the days of Shagmar son of Ananth,
  in the days of Jael, the highways were abandoned;
  travelers took to winding paths.
  Villagers in Israel would not fight;
  they held back until I, Deborah, arose,
  until I arose, a mother in Israel.

Thanks to Deborah and Jael, Israel found its way to an
awesome victory. The result was a long song, celebrating
the way in which they were strategic in battle. Before
Deborah, Israel was falling apart. Life stopped, highways
weren't utilized, and villages stopped living and fighting.
Thanks to these women, Israel moved from destitute to
powerful.
    There are many who suggest Deborah arose in
leadership because there were no men to do the job, but
the passage here proves otherwise. Deborah was not
chosen as a fill-in or because others were incompetent,

but because she was the most competent, most equipped person to arise for the job. Deborah was appointed to be the mother of Israel, because at that point in time, Israel needed a mother.

Judges 5:8-18:

God chose new leaders,
  when war came to the city gates,
but not a shield or spear was seen
  among forty thousand in Israel.
My heart is with Israel's princes,
  with the willing volunteers among the people.
Praise the LORD!

"You who ride on white donkeys,
  sitting on your saddle blankets,
  and you walk along the road,
consider the voice of the singers at the watering places.
  They recite the victories of the LORD,
  the victories of His villagers in Israel.

"Then the people of the LORD
  went down to the city gates.
Wake up, wake up, Deborah!
  Wake up, wake up, break out in song!
Arise, Barak!
  Take captive your captives, O son of Abinoam!'

"The remnant of the nobles came down;
  the people of the LORD came down to me against
    the mighty,
Some came from Ephraim, whose roots were in Amalek;
  Benjamin was with the people who followed You.
  From Makir captains came down,
  from Zebulun those who bear a commander's staff.
The princes of Issachar were with Deborah;
  Yes, Issachar was with Barak,
  sent under his command into the valley.
In the districts of Reuben
  there was much searching of heart.
Gilead stayed beyond the Jordan.

And Dan, why did he linger by the ships?
Asher remained on the coast
   and stayed in his coves.
The people of Zebulun risked their very lives;
   so did Naphtali on the terraced fields.

God knew a warring woman was necessary to lead the people of Israel. A team of warring women was needed to bring this nation to where it needed to be. In the text, I love the command, "Wake up, Deborah!" What I want to say to all of you here is, "Wake up, (insert your name here)!" Your inner warrior is in there, waiting and ready to stand up. Just like Deborah and Jael were needed for victory in their day, so this day needs you to stand up and do what is needed.

How many of us are out there, missing our blessing to stand up like Jael and Deborah and receive what God has for us in full, not in part? What are we missing out on for future generations, for others around us, for the future of our communities and our church?

If we want to be women who win, we need to embrace the stands of Deborah and Jael and be aggressive enough to get it. There are some things in your life that you need to kill (not people, not literally, but maybe some bad habits or bad relationships) and destroy and let them be gone from your life. What about that relationship you still hold on to, years after God told you that you were done with it? What about the bottle you keep drinking from or the pills you know you shouldn't be taking? What about that spending habit God has been dealing with you about for years? What about the anger God told you to let go of, but you keep holding on just in case someone decides to apologize? What about those fleshly appetites, attitudes, and desires you keep indulging that you keep feeding because you think it's fun at the time? What about the disrespect that creeps up, usually when you feel conviction? How about that anger, hatred, and bitterness you harbor for things long past? We wonder often why we don't have victory or aren't blessed, but in looking at some of the things on this list, is it any wonder? We keep letting Sisera live and not only live, run all over our lives and have the full reign without killing these issues dead and moving forward.

Warring women win because they go after what needs to be gotten, kill what needs to die, and stand victorious in the end. They are self-aware enough to recognize strengths and weaknesses, and work through one to conquer the other. They recognize God has brought so much to pass, just through their willingness to be determined to go and get it!

An aggressive faith leads to victory

Judges 5:19-31:

Kings came, they fought
  the kings of Canaan fought.
At Taanach, by the waters of Megiddo,
  they took no plunder of silver.
From the heavens the stars fought,
  from their courses they fought against Sisera.
The river swept them away,
  the age-old river, the river Kishon.
  March on, my soul; be strong!
Then thundered the horses' hooves –
  galloping, galloping go his mighty steeds.
'Curse Meroz,' said the angel of the LORD.
  'Curse its people bitterly,
Because they did not come to help the LORD,
  to help the LROD against the mighty.'

"Most blessed of women be Jael,
  the wife of Heber the Kenite,
  most blessed of tent-dwelling women.
He asked for water, and she gave him milk;
  in a bowl fit for nobles she brought him curdled milk.
Her hand reached for the tent peg,
  her right hand for the workman's hammer.
She struck Sisera, she crushed his head,
  She shattered and pierced his temple.
At her feet he sank,

he fell; there he lay.
At her feet, he sank, he fell;
  where he sank, there he fell – dead.

"Through the window peered Sisera's mother;
  Behind the lattice she cried out,
'Why is his chariot so long in coming?
  Why is the clatter of his chariots delayed?'
The wisest of her ladies answer her;
  indeed, she keeps saying to herself,
'Are they not finding and dividing the spoils:
  a woman or two for each man,
colorful garments as plunder for Sisera,
  colorful garments embroidered,
Highly embroidered garments for my neck –
  all this as plunder?'

"So may all your enemies perish, LORD!
  But may all who love You be like the sun
  when it rises in its strength."

Then the land had peace forty years.

One thing the song of Deborah and Jael does is show us that when God calls a woman to the victory, a man cannot do the work assigned to a woman. Jael was blessed – most blessed among all the women of the tents, of all the nomadic women of her time – because she had no fear to do what was needed. She wasn't afraid to kill what it was time to kill, and she was not afraid to be aggressive in the right situation.

I am sure there were some who didn't find Jael's actions so notable, even back then. There was someone who was angry they didn't get the victory (I bet Sisera's mother probably had a pretty dark opinion of the events of the day!), and even more angry that the victory went to a woman. Some mused about the unfairness of it all, as the song of Deborah and Jael continued to be sung. I don't think Jael particularly carried, nor worried about who was upset. She had her tent peg, she had her hammer, and she knew it was time to do what needed to do.

Now it's time for you to do what you need to do, so your faith can lead to victory.

Reflections

- What enemies need to be "killed" in your life?

- How do you feel about a woman being aggressive, versus vindictive?

- How can you relate to Deborah and Jael's story and experience?

CHAPTER FOUR

Eve

- Mother of All Living -

AND THE LORD GOD SAID TO THE WOMAN, WHAT IS THIS YOU HAVE DONE?
AND THE WOMAN SAID,
THE SERPENT BEGUILED (CHEATED, OUTWITTED AND DECEIVED) ME, AND I ATE.
(GENESIS 3:13, AMPC)

I am the youngest child in my family, which means my siblings were first to do everything before me. Whether it was go to school, learning to read, drive, date, graduate school, get married, or have a career, everyone was always ahead of me. By the time I was born, all my sisters had been to school, learned how to read, most were beyond elementary school, two of them had already been to college and one was engaged to be married! When you are the last to do everything, firsts seem intriguing, important, essential, and even a little forbidden.

Eve was the first woman ever, which means she was the first woman to do everything that pertained to life as we know it. She was the first to live, walk, talk, experience a relationship, have sex, have children, work hard, experience God, live with other people, get old, and eventually die. No woman experienced as many "firsts" as Eve, and no woman will again, because she was literally the first, the oldest, and the only one with original purpose.

It's unfortunate we don't hear more about this side of Eve when she comes up in Christian teaching. We hear about Eve, but unfortunately, a lot of what we hear about Eve is incorrect. Eve has been permanently stigmatized in the church as the ultimate bad girl, for whom no redemption is possible. By proxy, it is taught this has been passed to every woman, and that every woman, in the image of Eve, has these qualities.

If we stop and look at Eve, however, we can see that Eve received a bad reputation that, in most ways, is very, very unjustified. I'm not here to minimize Eve's role in the fall of humanity or to say Eve was without responsibility for what happened, but one very relevant thing we can't deny if we look at Eve is that we see Eve taking more responsibility than is hers to bear and Adam is treated as a victim without responsibility. This means we don't see Eve as blessed, and we miss the important blessings that were bestowed upon Eve, one who was blessed before any other woman on this earth.

Women in the time of Eve

Genesis 2:15-24:

The LORD God took the man and put him in the Garden of Eden to work it and take care of it. And the LORD God commanded the man, "You are free to eat from any tree in the garden; but you must not eat from the tree of the knowledge of good and evil, for when you eat from it you will certainly die."

The LORD God said, "It is not good for the man to be alone. I will make a helper suitable for him."

Now the LORD God had formed out of the ground all the wild animals and all the birds in the sky. He brought them to the man to see what he would name them; and whatever the man called each living creature, that was its name. So the man gave names to all the livestock, the birds in the sky and all the wild animals.

But for Adam no suitable helper was found. So the LORD God caused the man to fall into a deep sleep; and while he was sleeping, he took one of the man's ribs and closed up the place with flesh. Then the LORD God made a woman from the rib he had taken out of the man, and he brought her to the man.

The man said,

"This is now bone of my bones
   and flesh of my flesh;
she shall be called 'woman,'
   for she was taken out of man."

That is why a man leaves his father and mother and is united to his wife, and they become one flesh.

Since Eve was the first woman, all we know about women in her time is through these verses in the Bible. In the very beginning, humanity was found in one person, Adam. In realizing the need for companionship, from the one, God created two beings, Adam, and now Eve. She was part of Adam, taken to create a camaraderie and union that couldn't be achieved when they were one being. Far from being a secondary figure, she was there, suitable to provide something to and for Adam that the rest of life on earth couldn't provide. She lived in paradise, the Garden of Eden. Life was perfect, up until the fall of humanity. She didn't deal with the crazy restrictions or customs that we see evolve later in time. Eve enjoyed freedom, equality, and purpose, all until the time when a conversation with a snake changed her entire life.

The importance in seeing Eve as blessed

When you were growing up, how did your mother see herself? Was she always saying that she was fat or ugly when you were in earshot? Did you have a mom who was always on a diet, or trying out a new fad to look younger? Was she critical of herself, her value, and her self-worth?

If you had a mom like this, how did it make you feel? It, most likely, made you feel bad for your mom, like there was something wrong with her and you couldn't help her with it. Stepping back, how did it make you feel about yourself? When you looked in the mirror, were you critical of features that you have? When someone picked on you about something at school, was it all you could think about? How long was it before you reached a certain age, and you started "pinching an inch" on your own body or feeling insecure about how you look?

There have been many studies proving the critical eye our mothers have for their own bodies is a behavior that we, as girls, pick up ourselves. How our mothers look at themselves affects how we look at ourselves. It influences our thought processes about our bodies in negative ways.

I don't think it's that foreign – or outlandish – to suggest if our mothers can influence the way we view our own selves, the way we view Eve also effects how we consider ourselves as women. If all we hear about the first woman who ever lived is negative, critical, offensive, and downright sinister, we are going to feel that way about ourselves as her daughters. If our original mother portrayed is evil, then we are going to think we are all evil, too. The underlying idea that women are somehow deliberately sinful, temptresses, forbidden, hating, and disobedient passes down to every woman who has spent any time at all in church. No matter what anyone might want to say, I do believe this attitude does play a role in how we perceive ourselves and our own salvation, especially when we give women the message that they aren't salvageable or purposeful without a man, on their own, through Christ.

Proverbs 14:1:

The wise woman builds her house,
  but with her own hands the foolish one tears her down.

Laugh if you must to ease your discomfort, but if you think about portrayals of Bible women, they don't tend to be the most positive of viewpoints. Bible women are often a picture in extremes: they are either portrayed as so virtuous it's impossible to live up to their example, or they are so negative, nobody wants a similar association. Think about it. Mary is "pious and holy." Esther is "virtuous and brave." Ruth is "patient and devoted." There's nothing wrong with these observations, but these portrayals often lend nothing to them as real people. Like the rest of us, they had bad days, they occasionally did the wrong thing, and they definitely weren't the people we portray them to be in church. They were people and they did have amazing experiences and incredible fortitude, but that doesn't mean they walked around with a halo over their heads. Couple this contrast with the way we typically hear about women in church: comparing people to Jezebel, accusing Bathsheba of seducing David (wasn't the way it happened), degrading the woman at the well who spoke with Jesus, or calling people out as spiritual prostitutes or whores all give us certain perceptions of who we are and what we think God thinks of us.

For us to truly see ourselves as blessed, we need to see our original mother, Eve, as most blessed. She was blessed; it's not a myth or something we must contrive or make up. Her blessedness passes to us as do the consequences of sin. Her blessing tells us we can indeed overcome sin through Christ, and we need to embrace that to weed out the voices that tell us we can't be blessed. We need to change our understanding of Eve so we can change our understanding of ourselves.

The perfect duo, perfectly blessed

If you have never read the creation story in its entirety, I encourage you to do so. In reading these first few chapters of Genesis, do a little cross translational study and read it in at least three different translations, to gain different perspectives on its contents. It's an important and purposeful read for everyone who believes in God to see the carefully executed process of creation. I'm not one to get into the long-winded debates about timelines and when exactly everything took place, because I don't believe that's why the Genesis accounts of creation were written. Genesis doesn't exist to provide a scientific or technical explanation of creation. They are there to inspire our faith, to help us see God's hand in all that is around us, and to make us realize that as a part of God's creation, we too are a part of a bigger, grander plan than we could ever imagine.

Genesis 1:26-31:

Then God said, "Let Us make mankind in Our image, in Our likeness, so that they may rule over the fish of the sea and the birds in the sky, over the livestock and all the wild animals, and over all the creatures that move along the ground."

So God created man in His own image,
in the image of God He created Him;
male and female He created them.

God blessed them and said to them, "Be fruitful and increase in number; fill the earth and subdue it. Rule over the fish of the sea and the birds in the sky and over every living creature that moves on the ground."

Then God said, "I give you every seed-bearing plant on the face of the whole earth and every tree that has fruit with seed in it. They will be yours for food. And to all the beasts of the earth and all birds in the sky and all the creatures that move along the ground – everything that has the breath of life in it – I give every green plant for food." And it was so.

God saw all that He had made, and it was very good. And there was evening, and there was morning – the sixth day.

Because this book is not specifically about creation, I

don't want us to deviate too much from the topic at hand and cover the entire account of creation. At the point in the verse above, God already created everything we know in the world, right up to the creation of humanity, which consists of the spectrum from male to female. We often think this passage is just about Adam and that Eve came later, but Genesis 1 dispels this notion. All human beings (women included) are created in the image of God and are part of humanity, equal in the sight of God. Adam and Eve started out on an equal, even keel before God, and they were both blessed equally before God. There is no greater or lesser help in this relationship, no one who is more or less important.

More than the debates we tend to add to the examination of Adam and Eve (which aren't found in the Biblical text, by the way), there was a purpose to this specific creation, and this specific blessing. Being made in the image, or likeness of God endows humanity with reason, the ability to make decisions, choices, analyze circumstances and facts, live by intellect, faith, reason, and most of all, experience life beyond mere instinct. This means that humanity, from the beginning, was not simply programmed to follow certain instincts, regardless of the circumstances.

For example: A fish is going to follow a certain course of its own life cycle throughout its life. It can't sit down and decide it doesn't want to be a fish; it wants to be a frog instead. A fish doesn't have the capability to try and be a different type of fish, doing things differently from other fish. Human beings, however, have the capacity to sit down and decide what they want to do and who they want to be. This is the crux of being created in the image of God.

All humanity, therefore, has these same intellectual, faithful, and reasonable capacities, at least to some ability. The physical differences among genders does not change the aspects of God's image within us that pertain to areas of intellect and the ability to reach out to God and communicate or work effectively with one another. Physical differences and characteristics different aspects of the nature of God: the ability to create life, live strong, and be balanced between nurturing and strength. When we look at things like this, we understand a lot more about the relationship between people and our goal, which we are supposed to reach together: to reflect a type of the nature and love of God in our own relationships.

Unfortunately, many are so busy trying to pursue the notion of having "gender roles" that we aren't reflecting this kind of purpose in our relationships. Instead, we see conflict, strife, anger, and embitterment. We make life a competition instead of a joint venture, and this makes women feel inferior and men feel superior. If we are true students of the Bible, neither is true, and neither approaches the humility we are called to have as believers in Christ.

All of humanity (specifically in the beings of Adam and Eve) were blessed as a unit. At the same time, God also blessed male and female, as the entire spectrum that exists between them still reflects Him in His image. It says God blessed "them," not God blessed "him." We all have God-given authority, and that is one of the major results of divine blessing. The authority and dominion given to Adam was also given to Eve − it was not given to one over the other or in place of the other. Thus, just as she was, in the image of God, Eve was blessed.

Accepting ourselves as beautiful

Eve was blessed along with Adam because she, too, reflected the nature and image of God, just as she was. She was blessed, happy, fortunate, and to be envied because she was different from Adam and yet equal in every way. Being a woman is a special thing, and there are too many people who try to take the specialness out of it because they are threatened by it. No matter how hard they try, it doesn't change the fact that as a female of the Most High, you, we, all of us, are special.

Ezekiel 16:14:

You became famous in every nation because of your

beauty. Your beauty was perfect because I gave you My glory, declares the Almighty LORD. (GW)

When we truly embrace ourselves as being just as much in the image of God as anyone else in our lives also is in that same image, there is nothing that can ever stop us, make us feel inferior, or beneath anyone this side of heaven. By doing this, we know and embrace the essence of who we are. If we accept that we, as women, are blessed, then anything is possible. This is truly why, in many instances, there are people who don't want us to discover that power. Women bring forth life and think about the power in life: it is a force of creativity, inspiration, nature, intelligence, and authority. That is blessed, as it is a blessed thing to be a woman because of how God has created us. In our very nature, our very gifts, and the fruit that those gifts bear, we are always most blessed.

As for how we perceive ourselves in our physical image: we've heard for years that it's what "on the inside that counts." No matter how much we are told this, I think we know it's a lie from a worldly perspective. People tell us this because they hope it will make us less vain and more interested in our character, but it's not working. We still fall into the trap of spending millions of dollars annually for enhancements, treatments, and other appearance-based products to make us look more like we think we "should." All one must do is walk down the street and see how people stop and stare at a woman who is heavier, ogling a woman who is deemed attractive, or degrade a woman who is disabled or what society deems "unattractive."

All women are beautiful as the image of God. We spend too much time trying to fit into an abstract mold of beauty that the world has set up, but we forget that women reflect the beauty of God. This is true no matter what our dress size is, no matter what number the scale reads, and whether we are wearing a skirt or pants. We don't need to look like a model; we need to look like ourselves. If society isn't quick to see the beauty in us, our Father in heaven is, and we can trust He will send people into our lives who will recognize the awesome beauty within us, just as we are created.

Is it relevant that woman was declared "blessed?"

Some might argue that I am reiterating or exaggerating a point, but I'm not really interested in that argument. The truth is the truth: woman was declared blessed, and I don't think we hear it enough. We don't seem to get upset when we're told about prosperity for the tenth time, nor do we bat an eye when we hear derogatory messages about women incessantly. Yet whenever we talk about something elevates the women of God, we are often met with opposition.

In Adam and Eve, we see a powerful unity. They were blessed together, and they were blessed as themselves. This means they were still themselves, still unique and blessed in their individual attributes and reflections of God. This is important because we often mistake oneness for sameness. We think that to be one in the church or to even be one in marriage or with a spouse, we must have the same politics, viewpoints, and thoughts about everything. If we are blessed together and blessed as individuals, that means Scripture dispels this idea.

Adam and Eve were one, but they were not the same. The fact that God acknowledges this, and calls "female" blessed, all on her own, erases any possible notion that men are superior to women or women inferior to men. Even in their different reflections of God's image, women are just as blessed as men and given the same exact authority, commands, and dominion as men. So, we can understand that the notions we have about women in society — and often in the church and home, too — do not come from God, they come from the world.

This calls for a change in how we look at Eve and what happened with her, and how we look at all women since. We need to look at women, not as a weaker sex in capability, but with respect and honor as an equally blessed reflection of the image of God. By calling the first woman blessed, all attributes which make up a woman are, therefore, also blessed, and our very lives are established as special, happy, and fortunate to be envied. Unfortunately, many women don't live like this and never come to the point of this realization. We so often don't accept what God says about being a woman but listen to the voices of the world that put us down.

Woman of God, do you have any idea who you are and how fearfully, wonderfully, and blessed God has made you, just by being who you are and walking in His image? He has not created you to be a victim, a slave, to have no identity, live depressed, unfulfilled, or be abused. That is not who God has created you to be!

I Corinthians I I:2-I 6:

I praise you for remembering me in everything and for holding to the traditions just as I passed them on to you. But I want you to realize that the head of every man is Christ, and the head of every woman is man, and the head of Christ is God. Every man who prays or prophesies with his head covered dishonors his head. But every woman who prays or prophesies with her head uncovered dishonors her head − it is the same as having her head shaved. For if a woman does not cover her head, she might as well have her hair cut off; but if it is a disgrace for a woman to have her hair cut off or her head shaved, then she should cover her head.

A man ought not to cover his head, since he is the image and glory of God; but woman is the glory of man. For man did not come from woman, but woman from man; neither was man created for woman, but woman for man. It is for this reason that a woman ought to have authority over her own head, because of the angels. Nevertheless, in the Lord woman is not independent of man, nor is man independent of woman. For as woman came from man, so also man is born of woman. But everything comes from God.

Judge for yourselves: Is it proper for a woman to pray to God with her head uncovered? Does not the very nature of things teach you that if a man has long hair, it is a disgrace to him, but that if a woman has long hair, it is her glory? For long hair is given to her as a covering. If anyone wants to be contentious about this, we have no other practice − nor do the churches of God.

The passage I have cited above doesn't automatically seem to go with what we are talking about, but I selected it for an important reason. It is so important that we, as women, see the blessedness that exists in being a woman. We also need to surround ourselves with friends, other people, and leaders in our lives who reflect the blessedness they see. We can't choose our fathers or our other immediate male relatives, and sometimes men who seem like good choices at the time don't turn out to be as good as we thought they would be. This doesn't change the fact that we can choose our friends of all genders, leaders, potential mates, spouses, and we can establish how the men in our lives will treat us. It's important we set a good example with the men we know for our sons and our daughters, so they know how important it is to be a blessed woman of the Most High.

The cultural implications found in I Corinthians 11 don't imply that women are downgraded, nor that they are not important. The discussion about head coverings found therein is about culture − nothing more, nothing less − and about the spiritual virtue in dressing and attiring one's self within the expectations of one's culture, rather than standing out so much, people are unwilling to hear our prayers, our prophesies, or our message. Having one's head uncovered signaled prostitution, especially temple prostitution, in the Greek culture present at Corinth. Obviously, Christians didn't want to associate themselves with such conduct. Yet within this passage, we see something important: the Bible speaks of women having a sign of authority upon them, and as men and women not being independent of one another. Why? Because all things come from God, whether male, female, or something other or in between. It isn't spoken of in a subordinating capacity, but as a reality: we are one, and when we talk about the truth of blessing with one another, that means we are all blessed, all human beings (including female). No matter what sort of cultural concepts may exist, in the church, all Christians are one, not to be divided by Gender – and blessed if they are in Christ.

A good girl, gone bad...gone restored

Genesis 3: 1-6:

Now the serpent was more crafty than any of the wild animals the LORD God had made. He said to the woman, "Did God really say, 'You must not eat from any tree in the garden?'"

The woman said to the serpent, "We may eat fruit from the trees in the garden, but God did say, 'You must not eat fruit from the tree that is in the middle of the garden, and you must not touch it, or you will die.'"

"You will not surely die," the serpent said to the woman. "For God knows that when you eat of it your eyes will be opened, and you will be like God, knowing good and evil."

When the woman saw that the fruit of the tree was good for food and pleasing to the eye, and also desirable for gaining wisdom, she took some and ate it. She also gave some to her husband, who was with her, and he ate it.

Things went along just fine (at least so we know) in the garden until one day, Satan manifested through the serpent, who came unto Eve. The root of sin and the root of what happened in the garden doesn't rest with Adam or Eve, it rests with Satan. From the very beginning, Satan sought to distort the relationship God had with humanity, and I also believe the relationship that man and woman had with one another. If we understand this, we can stop trying to pass the blame back and forth between Adam and Eve. Both Adam and Eve did wrong, but more relevantly, Satan did wrong, trying to get people away

BLESSED THOUGHTS:

Whose fault was it?

Years ago when I was still in school, I was in a Bible class that wasn't particularly interesting (save some of the discussions we often had). One day, my (male) teacher said, "The Bible says we all sin because of Adam. But I don't know, maybe we should be blaming Eve!" Of course, every male in the class - at the ripe, young age we were — agreed. They cheered his perspective and formulated all sorts of theological positions (as if they really had any) to defend their opinions. I remember being very put out at the time but wasn't sure why. I didn't know much about the Bible back then and couldn't have formed much of a defense if I so desired. All I knew was that if they claimed to be so Biblical, they shouldn't be attempting to undermine the Bible with the eternal battle of the sexes (which, ironically enough, has its origins in the garden).

For many years, we've heard the story about Adam and Eve only from the view of what Eve did wrong. We don't consider Adam's role in things and, as a result, we easily believe what we hear about the topic. The Bible is clear in Romans that we all sin because of Adam's transgression, so where does that leave Eve? Was she just an innocent in what happened?

The truth about Adam and Eve is they show us two aspects that relate to sin, and we should pay attention to what the story tells us. Adam shows us about sin, because he was the one who disobeyed God. God gave Adam the instructions about not eating from the fruit of the tree in the Garden, not to Eve. Even though Eve seems to know of those regulations and, thus, should have followed them by proxy, she was not the one who had the responsibility of the rule. Therefore, she was not the one who led into sin. Eve was deceived, and she teaches us that deception can be just as bad as disobedience, even when we are accountable for our deception. Whenever we allow ourselves to be beguiled, to listen to Satan or other voices that turn us away from God, we allow ourselves to walk into a place of deception.

Simply put, it was both Adam and Eve's fault that sin came into the world, just through different measures. Adam sinned, but Eve allowed herself to be deceived. We see both parts of this component at work here: deception and sin play off one another. If someone can convince themselves long enough that something is a good idea, they will eventually do it. Deception nor sin are contingent on gender; anyone can sin or be deceived. The story uses both characters to illustrate the way that the two work in combination and lead away from the will of God.

Beyond the issue of accountability, I think we all need to step back and keep in mind that through the story of Adam and Eve (and then ultimately the fall of humanity into sin) that God's plan is clear and evident from the beginning to the end. If we are willing to see the passages from a deeper, more spiritual perspective, we will be able to see that in Eve, in Adam, and in their entire situation we see the promise of Christ, of the church, of redemption from sin, and an end to Satan's reign and influence over humanity. In the middle of the biggest catastrophe to date on the earth at that time, God still had an answer, a promise, and a solution. That should remind us that God is forever in the blessing business, even when we seem to deserve it the least.

from God.

Eve's first mistake is that she dialogued with the devil. In that discussion, she first lost her confidence in her blessed state. All of a sudden, she had all these questions and doubts about what she knew God had said. When she spoke what God said, somehow it came out radically different than what God had actually said.

In other words, Eve lied.

When we studied creation at Sanctuary Apostolic Fellowship (now Sanctuary International Fellowship Tabernacle – SIFT) originally in Raleigh. North Carolina, the question as to how Eve knew how to lie came up. I put forth the theory that I don't believe the time when Adam and Eve ate the forbidden fruit was the first time they thought about doing it. They were still people with free will, and I am sure they wondered about what God told them and why He gave them such a specific admonition. Over time, trying that fruit crossed their mind more than once, because they were still human. Had it not, it wouldn't have been so easy to play on Eve's thoughts and ideas to get her to take that fruit and try it out.

We learn from reading 2 Corinthians 11:3 that Eve

was deceived by the serpent:

But I am afraid that just as Eve was deceived by the serpent's cunning, your minds may somehow be led astray from your sincere and pure devotion to Christ.

Deception indicates Eve was beguiled by something. There was something that came along to distract her from fact, and she fell for it. Eve's deception was both about what God had told her about Himself and also what she thought about herself. Thus, we learn here that Eve's disobedience was out of deception, and it is very important to watch our dialogue and perceptions to avoid deception. We need to watch our mouths and our thoughts, to make sure what's in both is truly what is from God. We need to avoid the temptation to start distorting things given from Him because someone − or something − comes along to cause misperception.

Romans 5:12-14:

Therefore, just as sin entered the world through one man, and death through sin, and in this way death came to all men, because all sinned −

To be sure, sin was in the world before the law was given, but sin is not charged against anyone's account where there is no law. Nevertheless, death reigned from the time of Adam to the time of Moses, even over those who did not sin by breaking a command, as did Adam, who was a pattern of the One to come.

The Bible also tells us Eve gave the fruit to Adam, and he ate, too. Adam's disobedience was not out of deception, but out of sin. The serpent did not dialogue with him, thus Adam's culpability rests in that he did choose, willfully, to take the fruit. Eve didn't manipulate him into doing it or force the fruit down his throat. Adam was not a victim, but a willing participant.

Genesis 3:7-15:

Then, it was as if their eyes [the eyes of both of them] were opened. They realized [knew] they were naked, so they sewed fig leaves together and made something to cover [loincloths for] themselves [Rom. 5:12–21].

Then they heard the [sound of the] LORD God walking in the garden during the cool part of the day, and the man and his wife hid from the LORD God among the trees in the garden. But the LORD God called to the man and said, "Where are you?"

The man answered, "I heard You walking in the garden [Your voice/sound], and I was afraid because I was naked, so I hid."

God [He] asked, "Who told you that you were naked? Did you eat fruit from the tree from which I commanded you not to eat?"

The man said, "You gave this woman to me and she gave me fruit from the tree, so I ate it."

Then the LORD God said to the woman, "How could you have done such a thing [What is this you have done]?"

She answered, "The snake tricked [deceived; 1 Tim. 2:14] me, so I ate the fruit."

The LORD God said to the snake [serpent],

"Because you did this,
    a curse will be put on you.
    You will be cursed as no other animal, tame [beasts;
    livestock] or wild [of the field], will ever be.
You will crawl [go] on your stomach [belly],
    and you will eat dust all the days of your life.
I will make you and the woman
    enemies to each other [place hostility/enmity
    between you and the woman].
Your descendants [seed] and her descendants [seed]
    will be enemies.

One of her descendants [He] will crush your head,
and you will bite [strike; bruise; crush] His heel [Rom.
I 6:20; Rev. I 2:9]." (EXB)

God called out to Adam in the garden, who spilled the
beans as to what had happened with the serpent.
Without belaboring the story which we all know
reasonably well, God was looking for someone to be
accountable for what happened. Adam wasn't
accountable. He blamed Eve for what he did, and by
proxy, he also blamed God. By saying, "Hey look God,
that woman you put here with me is why I did this!" Adam
was also saying that God had responsibility for what
happened.

I've gone back and forth over the years about
whether Eve was truly accountable. If you have read
earlier works of mine, I probably said she wasn't. The truth
is that Eve's statement wasn't blaming or accusatory, and
she did state what happened. It's hard for me to read
whether she was accepting responsibility for what she
did. She admitted that she ate it, and she admitted eating
it because she allowed herself to be deceived by the
serpent. In that sense, even though Eve didn't outright
say, "I disobeyed you and I should not have done that,"
she was accountable. At the same time, she did assign
responsibility to the serpent, who was at the root of what
happened (which was correct). Deception indicates Eve
didn't understand the consequences of her actions
would invite. Sin indicates Adam knew he was doing the
wrong thing. Therefore, the reason why sin entered the
world through Adam, rather than Eve.

The serpent received the first penalty. We do not see
any promise, anywhere in the Old or New Testaments, for
redemption or for removal of the punishment placed
upon the serpent. Yet within the punishment placed upon
the serpent, there is a special promise tucked away in
there – not for the serpent, but for the woman.

Why is it specifically mentioned that there will be
enmity placed between the serpent and the woman?
First, the woman, Eve, was deceived that one time.
However, she clearly learned from her experience. A

woman who, even currently, comes to terms with beings deceived by a serpent (whether it is an abusive boyfriend, girlfriend, husband, father, stranger, or other person) won't allow herself to be deceived again. Most women have a strong aversion to all things deceptive and we make a strong stand in that against evil, because women are called to learn from their falls and their mistakes.

Eve was the first woman to learn from her mistakes. Is the penalty sometimes high for the mistakes we make? Yes, it is, but you better believe when we get strong in God and we stand up in accountability, we don't make them again.

Thus, by Eve's dialogue with the serpent and stepping up in accountability, women have all become the natural enemies of Satan. God has created us to be victorious in battle over the devil, and to win and overcome him. We have instincts that are God-given against Satan and his wiles, and we are ready and prepared to fight that battle.

The promise that we see further speaks of the offspring of the woman. The King James Version of the Bible speaks of the word "offspring" as "seed," which we all know in the natural realm, women do not have. This means the Bible speaks of a special birth, a special offspring, a special child, who would not be born of natural means. As Mary was also a woman, she was part of in Eve's lineage. Her Son, Jesus Christ, was the One born of woman and God, without a natural man, to crush the head of the serpent. The enemy struck His heel as a bruise, as something to try and wound Him, but Christ has the final victory over Satan, by destroying him.

Thus, women are a housing of Christ, as a type of the church. The church herself is feminine, which means in herself, Eve typified the church, heralding a time and a day when the church would protect and house Christ, follow His rule and love Him as our true Husband. Ephesians 5:25-32 says:

Husbands, love your wives, just as Christ loved the church and gave Himself up for her to make her holy, cleansing her by the washing with water through the word, and to present her to Himself as a radiant church, without stain or wrinkle or any other blemish, but holy and blameless. In this same way, husbands ought to love their wives as their own bodies. He who loves his wife loves himself. After all, no one ever hated their own body, but they feed and care for their body, just as Christ does the church – for we are members of His body. "For this reason a man will leave his father and mother and be united to his wife, and the two will become one flesh. This is a profound mystery – but I am talking about Christ and the church.

Even through Eve's confrontation with her actions (that might seem difficult or punitive), God promised redemption through the woman! What an amazing blessing!
Genesis 3:16-20:

Then God said to the woman,

"I will cause you to have much trouble [or increase your pain]
    when you are pregnant [in childbearing],
and when you give birth to children,
    you will have great pain.
You will greatly desire [the word implies a desire to
  control; 4:7] your husband,
    but he will rule over you."

Then God said to the man [or Adam; 1:27], "You listened to what your wife said, and you ate fruit from the tree from which I commanded you not to eat.

"So I will put a curse on [Cursed is] the ground,
    and you will have to work very hard [toil; labor] for your food.
In pain you will eat its food
    all the days of your life.
The ground will produce thorns and weeds [thistles] for you,
    and you will eat the plants of the field.

You will sweat and work hard for [By the sweat of your brow you will eat] your food.
Later you will return to the ground,
    because you were taken from it.
You are dust,
    and when you die, you will return to the dust [to dust you will return; 1 Cor. 15:21-22, 40-45]."

The man named his wife Eve [the name derives from an early form of the verb "to live"], because she was the mother of all the living. (EXB)

The way God addresses Adam and Eve in this passage is one of the primary foundations used to create confusion between men and women about their position before God. The only being who was cursed in Genesis 3 was the serpent. God never curses man or woman, and He never speaks of either one as being cursed. Rather, Adam and Eve are told they will experience the consequence of their actions. In the Hebrew, the labor and toil spoken of for both Adam and Eve is the exact same word. English translators specifically translate Eve's punishment as relating to childbirth, but the Hebrew doesn't indicate it is exclusive to or restrictive to this understanding. The truth of this world is that both bringing forth and maintaining life would be hard. Sin changed everything, including labor and work. Life, from sin onward, would be difficult.

In a sense, however, if we look at the fall of humanity and the consequences of sin, there is still a blessing lurking behind the scenes. Sin exists to drive us in a deeper way to the love of God and Christ. It has not been abolished because it should make us appreciate the love of God that never changes even more, embracing the forgiveness and the hope that lies therein.

As pertains to the second part of verse 16, we parallel back to our discussion on Eve as a prefigure of the church. If Eve was there, prefiguring the church for us and our relationship with Christ, then we will, as believers in the church, desire Christ, and He does rule over us. In the natural realm, however, it speaks of a darker warning, something that also relates and warns about deception. The men in our lives often do to us what Adam did to her: they break our hearts, abuse or mistreat us, or distort our image of ourselves to save themselves. God does not subject us to this. The promise of who we are must lie in Him, and not in our relationships with others. Where Jesus rules over us to righteousness, giving someone else that kind of control over us almost always leads us to heartbreak. In here, God was advising women, these types of the church who bear life, who follow Eve, to be cautious in our relationships, to make sure they are blessed in Him rather than deceiving by the world.

Finally, we are told that Eve is the mother of all living. She is not just the mother of other human beings, but she has a special relationship with all of creation, above all that lives. This is a blessing of life, of freedom, and a promise that life is, indeed, interconnected, in a special way within God's woman.

Neither male nor female

I have spent many years studying and teaching on Galatians 3:23-29:

Before the coming of this faith, we were held in custody under the law, locked up until the faith that was to come would be revealed. So the law was our guardian until Christ came that we might be justified by faith. Now that this faith has come, we are no longer under a guardian.

So in Christ Jesus you are all children of God through faith, for all of you who were baptized into Christ have clothed yourselves with Christ. There is neither Jew nor Gentile, neither slave nor free, nor is there male and female, for you are all one in Christ Jesus. If you belong to Christ, then you are Abraham's seed, and heirs according to the promise.

It might be interesting to some that I stick a verse in this chapter that says there is neither male nor female. After all, this is a book specifically for and about women. If we understand the verse in the context of the law of which it speaks, specifically to women, it gives us great freedom – both liberating Eve and us – and positioning us for a greater purpose in the church.

The Bible tells us that if we are in Christ, we are no longer prisoners bound by the law. While God's law was not totally burdensome to women (and in parts did espouse certain rights and freedoms that were not seen in other primitive cultures), its interpretation often created women who were prisoners to their fathers, husbands, male relatives, and, above all, to the concept of their regulations. The law's purpose was to make us aware we are sinners who need a Savior. It is exactly what I spoke of a little earlier: Sin exists to make us grateful, all the more, for the Father's love toward us. The law makes us aware that sin does exist, and it does hurt our relationship with Him. The good news is if we are in Christ, we are not bound to it any longer.

This means that if we are no longer "male or female" in Him, we have returned to the initial unity in the garden, where we found "humanity" rather than specified states for gender roles. We are called in Christ to rise above the roles, limitations, and the sinful heartache we experience in the pains of this life. We are better than the old person we used to be, because we have put on Christ. Now, we can become one and lift one another up, raising each other for the Kingdom and for the betterment of us all.

In Christ, we come full circle, reflecting that image He placed within us that has become marred by sin. We don't have to own who we used to be, anymore, because we have put on Christ and are a new creature.

I would definitely say this is, by far, the best blessing of all...and it all started way back when, in the garden, with our first mother, Eve.

Reflections

- What have you been told about yourself as a woman in church?

- How do you feel about Eve's experience?

- How can you relate to Eve's life and what we know of it?

CHAPTER FIVE

The Song of Solomon Woman
- Blessed by Love -

KEEP YOURSELVES IN GOD'S LOVE AS YOU WAIT FOR THE MERCY OF OUR
LORD JESUS CHRIST TO BRING YOU TO ETERNAL LIFE.
(JUDE 1:21)

I have never, in all my many years in church (which is a ridiculously high number now) ever heard a message from the Song of Solomon (sometimes called the Song of Songs)...let alone a message about this nameless, blessed woman in the Scriptures. I think the Song of Solomon makes us uncomfortable, especially in a church world that doesn't tend to see things in any form except the literal. What pertains to sex in the literal we reject, unless we think we can get a salacious, guilt-inducing message out of it. Because it is impossible to do this with the Song of Solomon, we reject it in favor of other passages that might be altered to fit our viewpoints more easily.

Regardless of the way the Song of Solomon is overlooked, the Song of Solomon is a very, very important book in the Bible for a variety of reasons. The primary reason: it is a type of our relationship with God and a reality that we can all have if we will apply God's love to our life and relationships. It makes the love of God flow within our lives in a practical way, in a way we can see in beautiful illustration and dramatic prose.

In the dramatic reading that is the Song of Solomon we find a man, a woman, and a group of friends. As the man and woman proclaim their love and excitement for relationship with one another, their friends celebrate their union. It was the woman in the Song of Solomon, however, who first caught my eye when I wrote my commentary, *Discovering Intimacy: A Journey Through the Song of Solomon* a few years back. She intrigued me because while we don't know her name and she is not mentioned as an example of faith in the New Testament, she is clearly blessed with something important and special that we should all aspire to recognize about ourselves and those around us.

Women in the time of the Song of Solomon woman

We don't know exactly when the Song of Solomon woman lived because we don't have a specific date for when the book itself was written. Scholars disagree about just when it was written, and that means there are a variety of opinions as to its time frame. What we can see clearly from the book itself and from the relationship between the woman and her male relatives is the way patriarchy influenced and frequently overshadowed her life.

Song of Solomon 5:6-8:

I opened the door for my lover,
  but my lover had left and was gone.
  When he spoke, he took my breath away [my spirit went out].
I looked for [sought] him, but I could not find him;
  I called for him, but he did not answer.
The watchmen [guards; an ancient equivalent to police; 3:3] found me
  as they patrolled [those who make their rounds in] the city.
They hit me and hurt [bruised] me;

the guards on the wall took away my veil [lifted my garments from me].
Promise me [I adjure you], women [daughters] of
    Jerusalem [1:5],
        if you find my lover,
tell him [what should you say to him? That] I am weak
    with love. (EXB)

Song of Solomon 8:8-9:

We have a little [small] sister,
    and her breasts are not yet grown [she has no breasts].
What should we do for our sister
    on the day she becomes engaged [is spoken for;
brothers were in charge of marriage negotiations]?
If she is a wall [chaste],
    we will put silver towers on her [support and honor
    her].
If she is a door [promiscuous],
    we will protect [enclose] her with cedar boards [put a
    stop to her sexual activity]. (EXB)

As a woman, the Song of Solomon woman lived in a culture that treated her as if she had no rights or personage as an individual. Echoing much of the concepts about "honor culture" we see in the Middle East and parts of Asia today, she was seen as a reflection of her brothers and other men such as the watchmen, and they saw fit to treat her however they wanted. The text goes as far as to imply rape, and overly state obvious brutality. This kind of treatment caused her emotional strife, hurt, and pain. Her lover became the opposite of the other men she had known. No matter how evil or oppressive a society may become, there are always people who choose to be different and love their partners in truth rather than in the ways that are comfortable for most to culturally interact. Regardless of what might be the norm, we always have the option to go against the tide and display proper care and relationship with our partners, reflecting a higher love than society will ever understand.

The realities about relationships − and us in relationships

We like to talk a good game about relationships, but I often get the feeling we don't have the first clue about them, not in the least. We rehash the same things we heard our ancestors say, not considering our ancestors had problematic relationships, just like we do. Just because grandma and grandpa stayed together 60 years doesn't mean they were happy, nor does it mean their relationship was stable. Statistics cite at least a quarter of all women will be in or have been in an abusive relationship, and I believe the actual statistic for abuse in relationships is quite a bit higher. Sometimes abuse doesn't take the form of physical violence, and that means there are women who have been in abusive relationships without visible scars who might not have even recognized they have been abused. They might have (or now know) that something didn't feel quite right, but they couldn't express what it was or what they perceived as being wrong.

Song of Solomon 7:9-13:

Let this wine go down sweetly for my lover;
*   may it flow gently past the lips and teeth.*
I belong to my lover,
*   and he desires only me [2:16; 6:3].*
Come, my lover,
*   let's go out into the country [to the field; a private place*
for intimacy]
*   and spend the night in the fields [villages].*
Let's go early to the vineyards
*   and see if the buds are on the vines.*
Let's see if the blossoms have already opened
*   and if the pomegranates have bloomed.*
There I will give you my love.
The mandrakes [an aphrodisiac; Gen. 30:14−16] give
*   their sweet smell,*
*   and all the best fruits [gifts] are at our gates*
*   [entrance].*
I have saved them [treasured them up] for you, my

lover,
 the old and the new [everything near and dear].
 (EXB)

The woman in the Song of Solomon was blessed for who she was, and she was blessed enough to have a partner who acknowledged the special, unique blessing on her life. Believe it or not, that is how God speaks to us and calls out to us, acknowledging what is important and special. We should have people in our lives who do the same for us, as well. The woman in the Song of Solomon was more than her past, more than what happened to her, and more than others might have thought of her. There is great truth in that this woman was a true overcomer. In being an overcomer, she was declared blessed by those who were closest to her and who mattered the most in her life.

More than anything else, I believe God shows us in the Song of Solomon that good relationships only work – they are only really good – if our mates see us as blessed and see the hand of God upon us, working through us and in us. Too often we pursue relationships for no other reason than we don't want to be alone. We can't fear being alone if we are going to be women who discover true blessing in life. We spend so much time trying to find blessing somewhere else or in places it doesn't belong, we walk into situations that aren't right for us in one form or another. If we can look in that mirror and see blessing (see what God is doing in and through us and love it for what it is), it will transform who we select to be in our lives.

Part of being blessed, happy, fortunate and to be envied is having that in our relationships. It has been my experience through many years of women's ministry and counseling women that most women don't find this type of experience in their relationships. Most women, especially those in ministry, face an uphill battle as the men in their lives don't see them as blessed, happy, or fortunate. They see them as cursed, damaged, and in need of male guidance. The Song of Solomon woman tells us that we deserve better, and that starts with how we perceive ourselves and with looking at ourselves with a blessed attitude. There's more to being blessed than things; there's also confidence, inner beauty, and an understanding of oneself that transforms us from the inside out.

Radiant in true beauty

I love the Song of Solomon because of its imagery. I can read it and see the couple talking back and forth to each other, doodling their names over and over again in their notebooks and daydreaming when the two of them are apart. When I see her face, what I see might surprise some. She doesn't look like a super model. She looks like you and like me. She's not perfect, just like we aren't perfect. But that's the point of unnamed Bible women: they are part of all of us. They are every woman in faith, who we are and who we are becoming as God transforms us.

Song of Solomon 1:2-8:

Kiss me with the kisses of your mouth,
   because your love is better than wine [makes one
   light-headed].
The smell [scent] of your perfume [cologne; oil] is
   pleasant [wonderful],
   and your name [reputation] is pleasant like expensive
[or poured out] perfume [cologne; oil].
   That's why the young women love you.
Take me with [Draw me after] you; let's run together.
   The king takes me into his rooms [bedroom; inner
   chamber].

We will rejoice and be happy with you;
   we praise your love more than wine [v. 2].
With good reason, the young women love you.

I'm dark but [or and] lovely [beautiful; she was out in the
   sun because her brothers forced her to work the fields;

v. 6],
   women [daughters] of Jerusalem [her friends whom she
is instructing about love],
      dark like the tents of Kedar [desert nomads; Gen.
      25:13; Jer. 49:28–29],
         like the curtains of Solomon [or Salma; south Arabian
         desert nomads].
Don't look at how dark [swarthy] I am,
      at how dark the sun has made me [because the sun
      scorched me].
My brothers [mother's sons] were angry with me
      and made me tend [or guard] the vineyards,
         so I haven't tended [or guarded] my own vineyard
         [referring to her body]!
Tell me, you whom I love,
      where do you feed your sheep [graze]?
      Where do you let them rest [lie down] at noon?
Why should I look for you near your friend's sheep,
      like a woman who wears a veil [like a prostitute going
      tent to tent; Gen. 38:14–15]?

You are the most beautiful of women.
      Surely you know to follow the tracks of the sheep
and feed your young goats
      near the shepherds' tents. (EXB)

The woman in the Song of Solomon is comfortable as much as she can be, because she is working out things within her. She is somewhat comfortable with herself as a sexual being, kissing her partner and being desirable and attractive. She is shown as being the instigator of romantic advancements, because she's not afraid to approach the one she loves. She does not fear rejection or denial of her advances. She is excited at the prospect of a physically intimate relationship, to shed her inhibitions and be with the one that she loves. She was not afraid to adorn herself, bringing out her best features, accentuating that which brought out her beauty. Despite the battle scars she has from her life, she recognizes herself as beautiful, more beautiful than we can fathom.

   Television, magazines, social media, and sometimes

even the church gives us a picture of what a "perfect" woman is supposed to be. If we listen to messages given in the pulpit (usually from men but sometimes even from women), there is a concept of how we are supposed to be as women in our intimate relationships. We're criticized for being less than ideal, less than perfect, or for being different. Perhaps one of the greatest disservices occurs when we are berated for needing healing when the healing we need effects our relationships or when healing changes how we perceive our relationships.

As people, we go through things that change our perspectives and change how we feel about ourselves and those with us. We look down upon ourselves in shame and we are ashamed of our scars. The woman in the Song of Solomon, however, recognizes her scars, and doesn't let anyone make her feel bad for them. The reference to her skin as being "dark, but lovely," isn't a racial reference, but an old belief that white skin was a sign of a life of ease, while dark skin was a sign of poverty (one had to labor in the sun and darkened skin from hours of labor in the sun). We don't understand this today, as many women spend thousands of dollars per year to look tan. In days gone by, it was far more desirable to lack tanned skin than to have it. We learn her darkened skin was caused by more than just having to work hard: it was caused because of familial injustice. Her stepbrothers, in anger toward her, penalized and abused her by forcing her to do their labor while her own property went into ruin. Her darkened skin was her battle scar; it represented what she went through in her life, and what she survived.

All of us have our own unique "darkened skin." They are things in our lives that somebody else can point out and notably see how we have been mistreated by someone else in our lives. We all have something we can stare at, pick at, or be upset about...but beyond all, those things in our lives stand to something far more important than beauty or attraction: they indicate we have survived.

Reflecting back true beauty

Song of Solomon 1:9-17:

My darling, you are like a mare
among the king's [Pharaoh's] stallions [driving them
crazy with desire].
Your cheeks are beautiful with ornaments [between
earrings],
and your neck with jewels [a necklace].
We will make for you gold earrings
with silver hooks [studs].

The smell of my perfume [nard] spreads out
to the king on his couch.
My lover is like a bag [sachet] of myrrh
that lies all night [lodges] between my breasts
[intimately].
My lover is like a bunch [cluster] of flowers [henna
blossoms; pleasant smelling and used to dye hair red]
from the vineyards at En Gedi [a romantic location
with a waterfall near the Dead Sea].

My darling, you are beautiful!
Oh, you are beautiful,
and your eyes are like doves [perhaps fluttering or a
reference to softness and beauty].
You are so handsome, my lover,
and so pleasant [or lovely]!
Our bed is the grass [green].
Cedar trees form our roof [the boards of our house];
our ceiling [rafters] is made of juniper wood [they find
intimacy outdoors]. (EXB)

The man in the Song of Solomon is a good man. Even though he is aware of her weaknesses and her hurts, he doesn't push those buttons in her life. He doesn't force her to be somewhere other than where she is, and he is not critical of her scars. He gives her the time and space to heal, to find herself and her needed voice, and her purpose, as she goes through her life with him by her side.

A wound that is continuously picked or opened never heals properly. The same is true of our emotional hurts. This woman could have lived with a man who did nothing but pick at her "dark skin," but she did not. There is something in this for all of us to learn, and for all of us to think about, both as women who are in intimate relationships and those of us who are in general relationships in our lives. We know that healing is an awesome and important thing in our lives, but there is something to be said for letting healing take place in its own time and function. Sometimes we are so in the faces of others about healing or getting healed (or maybe even in our own face) because we think it's blocking us from something else we desire. Lack of healing also gets the blame for all sorts of things, everything from blocking blessing to not being able to move forward in life.

Sometimes I think we put too much emphasis on things of this nature, as if confronting and dealing with things in a forced manner will get us in a different place sooner rather than later. The reality to healing is that there is a time and a season for all things. Some things don't move along as quickly as we might like, and that includes our healing process.

Picking, forcing, or aggravating healing in any situation does not make things better. When going through such a time, it's important to have supportive people in our lives. This is especially true when it comes to someone who serves as an intimate partner.

No matter how difficult things may be, we need to make sure our intimate partners reflect the beauty of God living within us. While we might not live in a world quite as poetic as in the day of the Song of Solomon, we are worthy as women of having an intimate partner that sees beauty and radiance within us at every pass. There should be no question as to how your intimate partner feels about you, or the esteem that they have for you. While not all partners are quite as expressive about their feelings, verbal acknowledgement of things such as your

BLESSED THOUGHTS:

Maybe we found love right where we are

Think, for a moment, about all the talk, associations, and things we hear about relationships (more specifically, intimate relationships relating to marriage or dating). All-too-often, it's just about the only relationship we hear about. People are told to anticipate it, want it, desire it, and that it will solve all the problems you've got. We don't talk about the basic principles of being good friends, of interacting with people, or general relationship dynamics. It's in-your-face, all the time, "Get married." "You need to be married!" If you're married and you're unhappy or having problems, somehow it's your fault – you need to follow this set of advice, this set of guidelines, be this kind of person. If the situation doesn't measure up, we assume it's the person...not the concept we have given them.

I've spent many years watching trends in relationships. In the past few years, I have noted how disconnected we seem in them, especially in relationships that, by virtue of their nature, tend to be more intimate. As a rule, people's expectations in their relationships are very high. We expect husbands and wives to be the end-all, be-all. We place such a high emphasis on relationships, it is virtually impossible for anyone to live up to the expectations that exist today. The more we place emphasis on marriage, not getting divorced, and on people being married, the more strain and more divorces we see. The more we push, the higher the rates are of people who are unhappy in their marriages.

One thing that goes along with this trend is the more we talk about marriage and by extension familial relationships, the more we get away from friendships and having friends outside of our most intimate associations. I know too many people who have virtually no friends outside of their marriage or immediate family, and this is hurting us. The more we expect our mates to fulfill more roles, the more we aren't getting those needs met.

When I found Ed Sheeran's song by pure accident one day, something about his line, "Maybe we found love right where we are" made my mind race. I wasn't familiar with Ed Sheeran before I heard his song, *Thinking Out Loud*. The video was a "suggestion to watch" on my YouTube feed while I watching the video of another artist. I watched it, not expecting much. Obviously, I got more than I anticipated.

The hit show *Friends* features an episode titled "The One

With the Two Parties." In it, Monica throws a birthday party for Rachel that gets quickly disrupted when both of Rachel's parents show up at the same time. The two are involved in a nasty divorce and are given to disrupt any event they attend together. In effort to save her birthday, the group takes on two parties, all to keep her parents apart. They deal with broken furniture, guests sneaking out of Monica's boring party to go to Joey and Chandler's party across the hall, Ross running back and forth to keep Rachel's father away from her mother, Joey kissing Rachel's mother to keep her from seeing Rachel's father, and the guys making general idiots of themselves, just to make sure Rachel's father can go between apartments without running into her mother. One of the best scenes was a discussion between Chandler and Rachel, where Chandler was able to sit and talk to her about having divorced parents, as his parents divorced when he was a child.

Rachel and Chandler never dated on the series. They were never more than friends who supported and cared about each other. Even though Ross and Rachel were dating at this point, the person Rachel needed to talk to in that moment was Chandler, not Ross. Ross understood that. He didn't get jealous, accuse Rachel of having an affair, or get angry at her because he knew who she was, and he knew that what she needed. At that moment, he couldn't offer her what Chandler could. As a friend, Chandler was able to help Rachel with what she was going through because he had been there. While Ross might have empathized, cared, even been attentive to her situation, he wasn't going to be able to give her what she needed at that moment.

As people, we need more than boyfriends, girlfriends, husbands, and wives. We need to be more than boyfriends, husbands, girlfriends, and wives in our lives, as well. There is more than one way to love someone, and more than one way to be loved by someone. Still neglected, our friends become our family and sometimes we have moments where the one who knows exactly what we need is not the one who is, according to popular culture, the one who is "supposed" to give it. That's why there is more than one person in the world, and it is especially why there is more than one individual in the world that cares about us and wants the best for us.

Genuine support isn't a "danger zone." It's not inappropriate and doesn't mean someone is going to run off and have an affair, break up their marriage, or do something otherwise socially unacceptable. While Ed Sheeran's song is clearly a love song and the individual is singing to his wife or girlfriend, there are principles in it that relate to strong support and friendship. Every one of us has had a friend that we truly cared about and knew cared about us and just took us and gave us a hug or reached out to us in our lives. We all have friends that we know will be with us no matter how old we get, who will be there for us to reach out with the touch of a hand, a hug, a good word, knowing that if we have them, we will never be alone.

As believers, we need to learn about love in our lives and all the ways we can reach out, just by being people. Love isn't just for marriage, it's not just for dating, it's for all our interactions with people. Maybe, just maybe if we come to reach out and learn about this beyond just the obvious, we might start to find some of what we need in this life returned to us because we've realized that what we are looking for there has been there all along. Instead of looking for things from people who can't give them, instead of looking for stuff all the time from one thing, we need to step back and realize that maybe we found love right where we are...where we don't expect it and are never looking for it.

beauty, attractiveness, and positive qualities should always be part of their routine encouragements toward you.

If you are in a relationship where you are always second-guessing your mate and how they feel, then that is a relationship that is not for you. None of us should have to beg for compliments or wonder where we stand with someone. Do we all have our bad days, yes, we do. Overall, however, your lover should look at you as nothing short of beloved. A woman cannot be comfortable in a relationship where she can't figure out where she stands with her partner, and that is true in communication, in life, and in the bedroom, as well.

Strength in truthful places

Song of Solomon 2:8-15:

I hear my lover's voice [the sound of my lover].
  Here he comes jumping [leaping] across the
  mountains,
    skipping [bounding] over the hills [he moves with
    agile grace and speed].
My lover is like a gazelle or a young deer [stag].
  Look, he stands behind our wall
peeking [staring] through the windows,
  looking through the blinds [lattice].
My lover spoke and said to me,
  "Get [Rise] up, my darling;
  let's go away, my beautiful one.
Look, the winter is past;
  the rains are over and gone [spring has arrived, the
  time of love].
Blossoms appear through all the land.
  The time has come to sing;
  the cooing of doves is heard in our land.
There are young figs on [ripening on] the fig trees,
  and the blossoms on the vines smell sweet [spread
  their fragrance].
Get [Rise] up, my darling;
  let's go away, my beautiful one."
My beloved is like a dove hiding in the cracks [crevices]
  of the rock,
  in the secret [hiding] places of the cliff.
Show me [Let me see] your face [form],
  and let me hear your voice.
Your voice is sweet [agreeable],
  and your face [form] is lovely [pleasant].
Catch [Grab] the foxes for us–
  the little foxes that ruin the vineyards
while they are in blossom [threats to the relationship].
(EXB)

There is a strength displayed between the woman in the Song of Solomon and her lover because of how the two of them feel about each other. They had the ability to express themselves fully, saying what they wanted to say to each other. It gives us deep food for thought because relationships today, if we compare them to this example of relationships, are very weak. Couples find themselves unable to talk or communicate, and many people get together for very wrong reasons: you are getting to an age where it's time to be married or you want to have children, you no longer want to be alone, or you think that being single is bad. You think they have a great car, a great house, a great set of abs, or not seeing anyone else coming along are not good reasons to get married.

We cannot pretend these different thoughts and feelings do not exist and give the same advice that didn't help the last generation to work these issues out. These complicated dynamics bring open wounds to the surface, strife and difficulties that are that much more of a hurdle to overcome.

Let me say this: I don't think it's impossible to make a relationship work if you've run into problems early in a relationship. I think it does make it harder, but I have seen some amazing transformations as God works within a couple, both as people and together, toward creating a true place of safety. That having been said, it's vital that couples are honest with each other. Love can't exist where there is no trust, and blessing can't flow without trust. This starts with being trustworthy within yourself: honest, clear, refraining from game-playing, and upfront about what bothers you, what you like and dislike, and what you truly want − and expect − in your relationship.

Being a couple who relies on the power of the verdant bed is a couple that knows intimacy, because they have found a place of trust. Getting married or involved for wrong reasons (or with the wrong people) means there will be problems, and that the blessing of God might not be visible or present. While yes, the "verdant bed" spoken of in the Song of Solomon does refer to having a good life intimately, it also means that they are able to find that place of trust, despite whatever they need to handle or overcome as people.

Intimate places should offer us safety and security, helping us to feel sheltered from the world and the judgments we often experience with one another (just like the cedars of Lebanon, pictured in Song of Solomon, chapter 1, as well).

The blessing of love

I Corinthians 13:4-7:

Love is patient, love is kind. It does not envy, it does not boast, it is not proud. It does not dishonor others, it is not self-seeking, it is not easily angered, it keeps no record of wrongs. Love does not delight in evil but rejoices with the truth. It always protects, always trusts, always hopes, always perseveres.

We've all heard preaching on I Corinthians 13 whenever a pastor or preacher wants to teach on love. Of course, yes, we should hear preaching on I Corinthians 13. In fact, I'd say we don't hear enough of it. Yet there are a few aspects of this chapter of Scripture that we often overlook.

The first is that I Corinthians 13 is not speaking of a romantic attraction, physical interest, or sexual drive. It's talking about *agape* love, one that reflects the highest aspiration or kind of love we can have. It's the love God has for us, and one that He asks us to have for all people, not just our intimate partners.

However, the fact that God requires us to have it for all people means we are to have it for our significant others. We cannot substitute other forms of love for *agape* and think our relationships – any relationship – will be successful. No long-term intimate relationship can survive on any other kind of love. While other forms are fine in addition to *agape*, a relationship can't survive without it.

Second, I Corinthians 13 reveals to us that love is a responsibility. It is something we do on purpose, translating to be a very big blessing in our lives as we give it and receive it. This means:

- If love is patient, we receive or give the blessing of someone's patience with us in a relationship, especially in situations where we are dealing with a wound or pain.

- If love is kind, that means we give and receive the blessing of kindness in a relationship, and that the relationship does not hurt either party.

- If love is not envious, then that means we give and receive the blessing of non-competition, not competing for gifts or dealing with unsupportive mates who are jealous of what either one has.

- If love is not proud, then that means we give and receive the blessing of a mate who isn't too proud to work together, to do what needs to be done in order to support the family and help with their relationship.

- If love is not rude, that means we give and receive the blessing of a relationship without contempt or disdain for one another.

- If love is not easily angered, that means we give and receive the blessing of a strife-free, peaceful relationship, without abuse or fear of violence.

- If love is not self-seeking, that means we give and receive the blessing of selflessness, trusting our mate with our well-being and giving them the same in return.

- If love keeps no record of wrongs, then we give and receive the blessing of living without grudges, feeling that we either will pay or must make someone else pay for the little mistakes they have made in their life with us.

- If love rejoices in the truth, that means we give and receive the delight in the good that happens in our relationships. We aren't happy when something bad happens to our partner, and we aren't angry when God brings good things into their lives.

- If love protects, trusts, hopes, and perseveres, then that means we give and receive an awesome series of blessings, right there, that we can't fathom its value!

What we can see as we step back and look over all these things: for love to be a true blessing, it must be more than just lip service, feelings, thinking someone is attractive, or having great sex. I think there's part of us that think it sounds good to say "I love you" all the time, but we never realize what those words mean and the blessing that should be attached with that promise.

One distinction I make when teaching about love is that it's one thing to love someone in the flesh, but it's another thing to truly love in and by the Spirit. As I pointed out earlier, there are different ways we can be interested in someone or "love" someone, based on different things that draw us to them. It's one thing to love someone's body, face, or physical appearance, superficially, in ways that will not last forever. It's a whole other thing to love in the Spirit and love someone for who they are and for the whole of what they are.

In the Song of Solomon, we see the unique dynamics of two people who truly had a love and depth for one another. I don't deny they spent hours and hours going on about how the other looked, but the odds are good that the two of them probably didn't look to other people like they looked to one another. The radiance of their love, of honoring and loving each other, made them beautiful to one another. They saw the Spirit within them, and they were inclined to follow that leading, wherever it took them.

Too many people do not reach the point where love becomes a blessing. In love, we give as well as receive, and if one is afraid to give true love, they are going to be afraid to receive it, as well. We don't understand it because the message to us is often distorted, we're told things are love that aren't, and then we aren't sure that love is something we genuinely want to receive.

If love is a blessing, then that should tell us to be blessed, it is something we will have in our lives. It is all the things we find above, and it is something that brings us back to the love of God, because God Himself is love.

Knowing when things are right

In looking at the blessing of love, I know that there are some reading this who are saying, "But Apostle, I want it in my life. How will I know if it's really there?" We've all been in and through situations where we were misled, where we thought we found true love only to kiss frog after frog and not find what we hoped was there.

Song of Solomon 4:7-12:

My darling, everything about you is beautiful,
and there is nothing at all wrong with you [you have
no blemish].
Come with me from Lebanon, my bride.
Come with me from Lebanon,
from the top of Mount Amana,
from the tops of Mount Senir and Mount Hermon.
Come from the lions' dens
and from the leopards' hills [apart from him she is in a
dangerous place].
My sister [an ancient term of endearment], my bride,
you have thrilled my heart [drive me crazy];
you have thrilled my heart [drive me crazy]
with a [one] glance of your eyes,
with one sparkle [jewel] from your necklace.
Your love is so sweet [How beautiful is your love], my
sister [4:9], my bride.
Your love is better than wine [makes one
lightheaded],
and your perfume [the scent of your oils] smells
better than any spice.
My bride, your lips drip honey;
honey and milk are under your tongue [sensuous
liquids that he will explore].
Your clothes smell like the cedars of Lebanon [the
best cedars].
My sister [4:9], my bride, you are like a garden locked

up [she has not been entered by a man],
 like a walled-in [sealed] spring, a closed-up [locked]
 fountain. (EXB)

From early on in their relationship, the man in the Song of
Solomon knew how he felt about this woman and that he
had to spend his life with her. He felt blessed with her,
blessed for having her in his life, and while it might not
have been from the first second he saw her, he had an
assurance that there was something in the relationship
that was right for him – and for her.

I've been asked if I believe in "love at first sight." The
truth is, I really don't. I believe that to develop love in a
true manner, it takes time. Part of showing love is making
the commitment to get to know them, about them as a
person and finding themselves at the end of it all with a
true knowledge and love for that person in a way that
transforms both of their lives.

However, I do believe in what I call the "inward
witness" about a relationship when the dynamics are
right. Even though someone may not love someone in
the sense of bringing forth the fullness of blessing right
away, they might have an assurance of peace and a
reassurance that pursuing this relationship is something
that they want to do.

An inward witness about a relationship doesn't mean
we know everything about a situation, nor does it mean
that every time we find it, a relationship will end in
"happily ever after." I totally acknowledge that sometimes
we aren't sure about things immediately in our
relationships. (Sometimes, we aren't sure about things for
awhile, and this is all right, too.) The assurance I speak of
is one of those things that if you've never experienced,
you won't know it until you do. I do know that when we
do find something that gives us that sense of purpose,
pursuit, and peace, however, that we need to pursue that
relationship, to see where it goes. It also means we
extend the basics of love while we wait for deeper things
to develop: patience, kindness, and attentiveness, while
we await the time when both partners recognize and are
ready to move forward, as in the Song of Solomon.

Seeing the result of that knowing is the anticipation of the blessing of love in one's life. We forget that sometimes being in a relationship that God is a part of is an incredible blessing, in and of itself. Just feeling that flow, that peace, that promise, and that gentle movement of the Spirit between people can be something that really empowers a person, encouraging them to take new risks, do new things, and launch into new places.

Seeing the image of God within you

In a later chapter in the Song of Solomon, we see the echo of friends who celebrated the work of God in this woman's life. It wasn't just her mate, although having a great mate in your life is a tremendous blessing. It was that favor, seen by her family earlier in time, that caused them to envy and punish her for what she had and who she was. Here we see she is unique, loved by her friends and her lover, and by those who truly see God at work in her.

Song of Solomon 6:4-9:

My darling, you are as beautiful as the city of Tirzah [onetime capital of the northern kingdom of Israel; the name means "pleasant"; 1 Kin. 14:17; 15:21],
*   as lovely as the city of Jerusalem [the capital of the southern kingdom of Judah; Ps. 122],*
*   like an army flying flags [awesome like an army under banners].*
Turn your eyes from me,
*   because they excite me too much [unsettle me].*
Your hair is like a flock of goats
*   streaming down Mount Gilead [4:1].*
Your teeth are like a flock of sheep
*   just coming from their bath [a washing; white];*
each one has a twin,
*   and none of them is missing [4:2].*
Your cheeks [or temple] behind your veil
*   are like slices of a pomegranate [reddish orange; 4:3].*

*There may be sixty queens and eighty slave women
[concubines; secondary wives]*
   *and so many girls you cannot count them,
but there is only one like my dove, my perfect [flawless]
   one.*
   *She is her mother's only daughter,
   the brightest [favored] of the one who gave her birth.
The young women [daughters] saw her and called her
happy [blessed];
   the queens and the slave women [concubines, v. 8]
   also praised her.* (EXB)

How are you unique? How are you special, uniquely
blessed and specially favored by God Himself? All of us
have been blessed and given certain gifts, abilities, and
talents to bear fruit in this life. There are things that make
the truly blessed woman special and notable, and yes,
things that others grow to love and celebrate about her.
We tapped into this before when we discussed Mary, but
the truth is that blessed women are different. They don't
just do what everyone else is doing, because that
approach is just too easy to coast through life. Blessed
women take the road less traveled, walk to the beat of a
different drum, and don't follow the same trail as
everyone else.

   Yes, this means there are those who think that such
blessed women are strange, crazy, and the like. Being
blessed makes us special and it reaps something that
being like everyone else can never, ever get us.

   I've been dealing with this issue in my own life for a
few months now. Just because I serve as an apostle
doesn't mean I don't hear from God or deal with Him
about things in my own personal walk. Believe me, God
and I are almost always having a conversation. As soon
as I am done with one thing, I am probably working on
something else, as I discover that transformation from
glory to glory and faith to faith is often in the form of
every step I take. You wouldn't believe how many people
I have met who, in one form or another, don't seem to
understand or "get" me on the level I hoped they would.
I've dealt with it from people I have covered spiritually, to

family members, to even those I have been in an intimate relationship with at times. It was an issue among those I led, the limited friendships I had, and in my first marriage. For years, I fought that difference. It was my own human reasoning that if no one was able to understand me, no one would want me as their minister or to work with me. As the years went by and I seemed to pile on far more rejections than acceptances, I started feeling like this was a problem that didn't have a resolution.

Through many different seasonal shifts, I've come to realize that not everyone who has come across my path has truly been an assignment from the Lord. I shouldn't have pursued every relationship that came along. Not everyone who has been around me was truly for me, and not everyone I involved myself with (both professionally and personally) could handle the kind of leader I am and the type of purpose that I have in my work. It takes a specific type of person to be under my leadership and a specific type of person to be in my life as a friend, acquaintance, or serious relationship. Recognizing this made me see the blessing that the ministry I have is for those who understand that and for the people who are in my life that truly do care about me. While it's all still a work in progress in many ways, I am seeing more and more that as much as I have to see the image of God in those who are around me, they too have to see — and understand that special Spiritual spark — within me, as well.

The power of love (both human and divine)

Within the blessing of love is the truth that nothing can quench it, nor diminish it for what it is. A true, lasting mature woman of God is going to recognize that just as love with God does not fade away, neither will the love of God leave us.

Song of Solomon 8:5-7:

Who is this coming out of the desert [wilderness; 3:6], leaning on her lover?

I woke [aroused] you under the apple tree
   where you were born [your mother conceived you];
   there your mother gave birth to you [the one who
   gave you birth conceived you].
Put [Set] me like a seal [leaving an impression on clay,
showing ownership] on your heart [inside],
   like a seal on your arm [outside].
Love is as strong as death;
   jealousy [or passion] is as strong [tenacious] as the
   grave.
Love bursts into flames [Its flame is an intense fire]
   and burns like a hot fire [or a godlike flame].
Even much water cannot put out the flame of love;
   floods cannot drown [flood] love.
If a man offered everything [all the wealth] in his house
   for love,
   people would totally reject it [or he would be
completely despised]. (EXB)

We all like to talk about love as long as it doesn't challenge us or take us to a place where we have to examine ourselves. The idea of love is endlessly appealing until we discuss what it requires of each of us. But the truth about love — even as a blessing — is that it must do just that to bring us to where God desires us to be as pertains to love. I'd venture that most don't allow themselves to go to this true place with love, because it is a blessing that changes everything.

This love changes us because when we start receiving it (especially in shadows and types through others in our lives), it brings us back to the love of God. The ultimate message we hear in the Song of Solomon is God calling us back with a perfect love, one that desires to bless us and transform us in a way that is beyond anything that we can ever imagine. Because of this, I think it scares us, and it causes us to push it away and push away God on some level. It's a transformation that brings us to contentment and helps us to stop wanting and pursuing all the wrong, comfortable things throughout our lives. We realize God loves us, sinners or not, and that through all that we have put God through in our lives, He is still there, and still with us.

Receiving this blessing helps us to be a better blessing to other people. I have noted over the past year, especially as I started dealing with the love of God and accepting it in every area of my life, how lacking we are in love today. We are so worried that telling someone about God's love will somehow enable them to sin that we are not conveying this essential and important message to the world. Love isn't about sin, it doesn't give permission to sin, and it truly does give hope that anything can be overcome (even sin). Being someone who has come to a place of acceptance of love of God and others helps us to empathize, to love deeper, to meet greater challenges, and to take on things in a powerful way so we can transform everything we touch.

True love isn't the mushy, romantic movies we see on television that don't apply or depict the truth of everyday living. It's something we are worthy of having, worthy of giving, and something we should want for ourselves and others. The time is now to reach out and take it, and let it change who we are so we can change this world.

You are the radiant queen!

Psalm 45:9-17:

Daughters of kings are among your honored women;
at your right hand is the royal bride in gold of Ophir.

Listen, O daughter, consider and pay careful attention:
  Forget your people and your father's house.
Let the king be enthralled by your beauty;
  honor him, for he is your lord.
The city of Tyre will come with a gift,
  people of wealth will seek your favor.
All glorious is the princess within her chamber;
  her gown is interwoven with gold.
In embroidered garments she is led to the king;
  her virgin companions follow her –
  those brought to be with her.

Led in with joy and gladness,
  they enter the palace of the king.

Your sons will take the place of your fathers;
  you will make them princes throughout the land.

I will perpetuate your memory through all generations;
  therefore the nations will praise you for ever and ever.

The Bible itself addresses us as royal, honored women, adorned and radiant. That nameless woman in the Song of Solomon is every one of us, rising up to accept what God says about us and who we are to be. It is not God's will we stay in abusive relationships, think of ourselves as ugly or unworthy, or that we accept second best within our relationship situations. It is fully His will that we embrace His image within each and every one of us, seeing ourselves as He sees us.

Sometimes the biggest barrier we encounter in receiving God's blessing is us, ourselves. We have to receive and cooperate with the work God wants to do within us and accept that work as a part of who we are. Rather than identifying ourselves through our hurts, our pains, and the things inflicted upon us, we must see the beauty God has created. When we do this, we will receive what those who love us most desire to give to us through love, we will embrace love in our intimate relationships, and we will desire to give love.

It all starts with accepting God's love toward us, and loving who we are, as ourselves.

Reflections

- In reading about the woman in the Song of Solomon, what do you notice about her?

- What do you feel the Song of Solomon woman can teach us about relationships?

- How can you relate to the woman's life in the

Song of Solomon and what we know of it?

CHAPTER SIX

The Proverbs 31 Woman
- Celebrating the Blessing That is Woman -

GOD IS WITHIN HER, SHE WILL NOT FALL; GOD WILL HELP HER AT BREAK OF DAY.
(PSALM 46:5)

AH, the Proverbs 31 woman. Some of you probably wonder where she's been all this time. Truth is, when I first put things together for this book, I wanted to find a way to avoid her. I have a deep, dark, Christian woman confession to make...

For the longest time, I did not like the Proverbs 31 woman.

Why, you ask? She sounded like a giant to-do list of perfect and epic proportions that was impossible to beat. Well, I certainly could not measure up to her vast list of accomplishments. The way it was taught to me, she was who we were to be if we wanted to be virtuous. In some way, she was always slightly out of reach. If we ever dared say we were tired, questioned that maybe some of what was presented in Proverbs 31 wasn't applicable in the same way today (who owns a vineyard? Not me!), or that maybe, just maybe we were missing something in our assessment of Proverbs 31...we were accused of something. Maybe we just didn't want to be "virtuous." The men in our lives wouldn't want us. Our parents wouldn't be proud of us...oh, the cataclysmic disasters that awaited women who didn't feel like they could be Proverbs 31 women...

Now it all sounds rather ridiculous to me. I was fighting a person I didn't have to become, because I was already a Proverbs 31 woman in my own right. As another nameless, Biblical woman – only this one is taken every way – she still represents every single one of us, the things we do well and yes, the aspirations we should have to be who God has created us to be in our character, empowerment, and diligence.

Women in the time of the Proverbs 31 woman

Proverbs 31 tells us it was written thanks to King Lemuel, a Biblical king. This should give us an idea of when it was written, right? Wrong. We have no idea when King Lemuel lived, because he was otherwise unknown. Some historians believe that because "Lemuel" means "belonging to God," the term is a play on the character of Solomon. Solomon reigned from 970 to 931 B.C. This gives us enough of an idea for a time frame of the book, even if Lemuel and Solomon were two different individuals and we don't have an exact date for the prophecy. The words were given somewhere before or during this period, and that tells us enough to look at what we need to know.

Solomon was a wise king, but throughout his reign, he strayed far from God into a world of 700 wives and 300 hundred concubines. Seen as a political statement (marriages and concubines were a part of treaties, agreements, and general politics between nations in those days), Solomon fell into idolatry because many of these women were from pagan nations.

I Kings 11:1-6:

King Solomon, however, loved many foreign women besides Pharaoh's daughter – Moabites, Ammonites, Edomites, Sidonians and Hittites. They were from nations about which the LORD had told the Israelites, "You must not intermarry with them, because they will surely turn your hearts after their gods." Nevertheless, Solomon held fast to them in love. He had seven hundred wives of royal birth and three hundred concubines, and his wives led him astray. As Solomon grew old, his wives turned his heart after other gods, and his heart was not fully devoted to the LORD his God, as the heart of David his father had been. He followed Ashtoreth the goddess of the Sidionians, and Molek the detestable god of the Ammonites. So Solomon did evil in the eyes of the LORD; he did not follow the LORD completely, as David his father had done.

I mention this because this information, coupled with what we spoke of as regards the time frame the woman in the Song of Solomon also lived, shows the way women were regarded as second-class citizens and often nothing more than mere property.

Wives were bought − concubines were acquired. The difference between a wife and a concubine was a dowry, or the ability to complete the financial transaction of marriage. Concubines existed for the purpose of male sexual pleasure, and children born through concubines were either adopted by the legally married couple or considered illegitimate. Concubines did not enjoy the same legal status as wives and could not inherit property.

This means women's marriages were still arranged. As a general rule, women worked hard in domestic duties (although they did have a niche in things such as midwifery) and most likely played a role in control of a household's material resources. We can also see the special role the queen mothers played in Israel. The mother of a king served official functions within the court of their ruling sons, and were influential in who might ascend next to the throne. (We will discuss this more a little later).

It took a special − and unique − woman to stand out from the rest of the crowd. We also see there were always special women who dared to be different and instill better and counter-cultural values in those who were part of the next generation after them.

The myth about the "ideal" woman

I spoke a little in the last chapter about the church's role in perpetuating the notion of an "ideal" woman. While before we talked more about it in a physical sense, the church tends to create an "ideal" woman in the context of what someone's (usually that minister's or speaker's) "ideal" woman is. I am not going to get into the extremely sexist nature of many of these messages. We never hear a sermon on what an "ideal" man is, or how a man can best serve his wife as a husband, or how he can bless or bring out the best in her (although it is obvious from what we have just discussed that there are passages in the Bible that speak on such topics). We never speak about an "ideal" partner of non-binary or genderqueer identity. The problem with this concept is that the "ideals" discussed specifically for women never agree. The messages tend toward contradiction, and no woman I have ever met in my more than 40-plus years of life on this earth measures up entirely. But what are some of these criteria? Maybe we should look at some of the different "ideals" that people seem to generate from the Proverbs 31 woman:

- Stay-at-home wife and mother
- Working woman who balances life perfectly
- Thrives in a home-based business
- Family is the center of her existence
- Runs to her husband with every decision she makes
- Diligent
- Not lazy
- Charitable
- Strong when needed, sensitive the rest of the time
- Proper
- Wise

There's no question the Proverbs 31 woman is a blessed woman, but I think the way she is sometimes perceived doesn't come across as such. She sounds burdened, confusing, complicated, and like she has things to do, from morning to night. Influenced by the world, we've taken the concept of an "ideal" woman and turned her into Proverbs 31, taking away the whole point of Proverbs 31 and why it exists in the first place.

Proverbs 11:16:

A kind [gracious] woman gets respect [honor],
but cruel [violent] men get only wealth. (EXB)

One of the most notable − and understated − aspects of Proverbs 31 is its rather militant tone. What we translate as "virtuous woman" or "woman of virtue" is actually translated as "valorous woman" or "woman of valor." This indicates that she was a woman who took charge of her life and won the battle for life, achieving something important and powerful within it. She made her life matter, in a way that only she could do so.

In Judaism, Proverbs 31 is understood by husbands to be a complete and powerful praise of their wives for all they accomplish and do on a regular basis. It's not regarded as a to-do list, but something that summarizes the greatness that is a woman and the greatness of all her abilities. It is a statement of wonder and awe, something the man in her life stands back and heralds how she is truly great and why he is lucky to have her. It's not about which specific things on that list she does or doesn't do, but more about celebrating her for who she is. In every line, he is thanking God for her.

Now if we could just hear thanks, praise, and appreciation for who we are rather than criticism for what we aren't when we read Proverbs 31. It's time for a Proverbs 31 reorientation.

The prophecy came from a woman

I think we fear excellence because in excellence comes judgment that should, rightly, make us uncomfortable. When we are told to be excellent or given a long list of tasks to do, it doesn't make us feel blessed; it makes us feel judged. In the case of Proverbs 31, we are being scaled and judged by a woman who is nameless and faceless. We don't even know her. It doesn't help when we walk into a church and start hearing about how "Sister So-And-So" is the "perfect model of Proverbs 31" when we know better. She might clean up nice at church, but she's a messy, nasty, extra woman at home and her kids eat cereal out of the box with a cooking spoon because she's too lazy to teach them how to make it for themselves. We know plenty of women who others think are the salt of the earth, but messy to no end in their personal lives. Yes, the judgment of Proverbs 31 is based on who looks the best part, and the reality is usually far from the truth. But this approach to Proverbs 31 also introduces an element into the mix that shouldn't be present in our churches (but all-too-often is)...

That would be competition. The way we interpret Proverbs 31 and use the model of a Proverbs 31 woman as some kind of trophy wife, mother, girlfriend, or church member introduces the spirit of competition as every woman tries to polish up just like her. We're missing the point. and the spirit of Proverbs 31. In place, we introduce another spirit, one that is worldly, nasty, fleshly, and judgmental.

Proverbs 31:1-3:

The sayings of King Lemuel − an inspired utterance his mother taught him:

Listen, my son! Listen, son of my womb!
  Listen, my son, the answer to my prayers!
Do not spend your strength on women,
  Your vigor on those who ruin kings.

I am starting with verse 1 in our look at Proverbs 31 because no one ever does. I've never even heard mention of Proverbs 31:1-9 in a message before. We act like the chapter starts with verse 10 and forget what comes before it. It turns out that, when we read what's written there, it's rather important:

The words of Proverbs 31, in its entirety, were the

prophecy (inspired utterance) of a woman, taught to a son. Not just any mother and son, but the queen mother of King Lemuel. As we mentioned earlier, queen mothers played a role in ancient royal courts, second in power only to the king himself. Her role was often advisory, serving as counsel to the king and advocating for the people before the monarch.

Saying this helps us understand the words, teaching, and purpose of Proverbs 31. It wasn't just an isolated, random passage, but one that reflected thoughts of the royal courts. Lemuel's mother (whoever she was) was teaching her son, one day to be both man and king, about the virtues of life and of the value in having a good woman in his life. She was teaching him the need to appreciate her and praise God for her. It had nothing to do with to-do lists, outdoing each other, or being extra. Because a woman said this to begin with, it was never meant to be burdensome. It was the words of a mother, looking out for her son, encouraging him to remember the importance of keeping a good character himself and encouraging his future wife.

Proverbs 31:4-9:

It is not for kings, Lemuel –
  It is not for kings to drink wine,
  not for rulers to crave beer,
lest they drink and forget what has been decreed,
  and deprive all the oppressed of their rights.
Let beer be for those who are perishing,
  wine to those who are in anguish!
Let them drink and forget their poverty
  and remember their misery no more.

Speak up for those who cannot speak for themselves,
  for the rights of all who are destitute.
Speak up and judge fairly;
  defend the rights of the poor and needy."

These early verses show us the important role mothers can play in the lives of their sons. It drives me crazy when we see post after post after post on the internet claiming that women are incapable of raising good men without fathers. I am the first to admit that the ideal for the family is a household where all parents are present and involved in the lives of their children. I am not questioning that children need a variety of role models and people in their environment who display the best of varying genders. I am also going to say that history is full of single mothers and unusual family situations; that didn't just start with modern times. Whether due to war, illness, abandonment, poverty, immigration, or a host of other things, women have raised male children just fine, on their own, for thousands and thousands of years. Their sons did not grow up to be psychopaths or have severe emotional problems. Children can grow up in any variety of family situations and turn out just fine. Mothers can do right by their sons without spoiling them and help them become the men God created them to be. It is wrong to think a mother needs to disappear from her son's life at some point in time so he can learn "how to be a man." The mother of King Lemuel took the time to teach her son the truth about being a man, with important advice about avoiding too much alcohol (and by extension, addictive substances), making sure he governed himself and his Kingdom well, and that he was an advocate both fair and just, able to speak up for the people. After discussing this, she makes sure he knows the importance in having a wife who is of good character and in celebrating her, just as she is, for all she does well and for how blessed she is. This is something that mothers need to do for their sons that a father can't give them: she can prepare him for a balanced life, one that is not void of love and consideration for others, and one that teaches him that as much as he might think he has it all, he doesn't have anything without the presence of those who love and support him in his life.

A warning against the wrong kind of woman

Proverbs 31:3:

Do not spend your strength on women,
  your vigor on those who ruin kings.

On a side note, Proverbs 31 doesn't just praise the right woman; it also mentions avoiding the wrong woman. Now wait, right? I said earlier there is no wrong way to be a woman, and that is a true statement in the sense that we should be exactly who we are created to be. It's not about looks, personality, or the things we desire to do as women. But it is still possible to be a "wrong woman" if you use what you have to be a source of temptation or cause other people to stumble in their lives. In this particular passage, I believe she speaks of women who are a temptation into adultery or prostitution, but the meaning of such, I believe, needs to extend far beyond just those simple boundaries. We can be the wrong kind of woman if our character leads others into evil, rather than good.

I am not a woman who feels the debates on modesty are fair to women in church. In fact, I think the entire concept that women are constantly given responsibility for male lusts, for male temptations, and for the way that men behave is ludicrous. That having been said, there are people (including women people) who seek to instigate other people: whether it's to sin, to rile emotions or feelings, or to stand in anger or hostility. Some women do this with the intention to gain prestige or control of others. There are women who try to get both men and other women away from their purposes in life and away from destiny. No matter who you are, such behavior is not attractive.

We all should check our behavior to see if we act as negative instigators or if we are drawn in by such. We are called to help one another in Christ and build toward good things, not tear one another down into nothingness. There may be behaviors you exhibit that are not of God, that do not help glorify God within you. If this is the case, it's time to look at those behaviors and work on changing them. As we are to be in Christ, we are to transform into a new person that we can't become if we keep holding onto things from who we used to be – whether it's stuff that happened to us or things that we persist in doing, even when we are supposed to be different.

We need to be uncompromising in our pursuit of righteousness in every form it takes and every way we operate. We should be people who take an interest in others, offering solutions to what goes on in the world, and I'm not talking as deeply as going out and being lawmakers or changing laws. I am talking about being the change you want to see in the world and making that difference in someone else's life.

We also need to speak up and judge fairly. This applies to every aspect of our lives, and we need to approach it with a good balance. There are times when we don't speak up and we should, times when we speak up and we shouldn't, and times when we just say the wrong thing for the wrong reasons. We need to beware talking about things we know nothing about, beware judgments, and beware using our speech for the wrong things.

This means we seek to be a blessing, add to the lives of others around us, and that the measure of our lives for others should be a precious, precious thing.

More precious than rubies

Proverbs 31:10-11:

A wife of noble character who can find?
  She is worth far more than rubies.
Her husband has full confidence in her
  and lacks nothing of value.

One thing we need to take into consideration in our understanding of Proverbs 31 – and much of what is specifically listed here – is in relation to royal imagery. If King Lemuel's mother was preparing him for adulthood and the responsibility of marriage, the type of woman he selected to be his bride was very, very important. Not just any woman could go before the king to become his bride. He needed to select a woman of fine character and praise that character repeatedly to both acknowledge and celebrate it in their marriage.

Marriage in those days, particularly with kings, was not just a social action or an emotional one. It was also political. Along with those politics came rules and regulations about the kind of woman that a king should have. As women today, very few of us will marry a political king, which means some of how we understand this passage gets eschewed when we try to take it in the context of modern life. If they are talking about royalty, then royal imagery is going to be used to bespeak of the wonderment that is present in this situation.

Nonetheless, as women, we still answer to a higher King: God, our Father. One of the things I teach the girls in our church is that if God is their Father and He is King, that means they are princesses because they are His daughters. This doesn't mean living like something in a fairy tale or a movie where we all break into song and spend our lives animated, in funny situations. Just as being a political princess in this world means doing certain things: being educated, conducting oneself in a proper manner, and being involved and interested in the world around us, we must do those things, too. We need to consider how we carry ourselves and how such appears before others, what that tells others about God, and what that says about us.

The same is true for us, even though we are now adults. Sometimes we get it in our heads that we are Christians, and we can act any way we want and have anything we want, if we put up the right church front and no one calls us out on our behavior. God has called us to be His daughters, not divas. As His daughters, we need to set ourselves to be excellent and valuable and find the way to be both excellent and most precious, given who we are and what God has gifted us with.

Let me also add, to alleviate any type of thought or idea to the contrary: you are not going to be everyone's cup of tea. Sometimes I have been shocked and offended to learn the people to whom I was kindest and did the most for are those who have, both behind my back and to my face, disliked me the most. What you have to offer – what is most valuable, precious, and beautiful – is not going to be understood by everyone or embraced by everyone. It doesn't make us bad; it doesn't make us wrong; it makes us different.

As women, we need to see ourselves as of immeasurable value valuable and embrace ourselves as important. If God reminds us that we are more precious than rubies, that should mean something to us. We make ourselves trustworthy and that shows in the heart of those who trust in us, because rather than seeing lack, they see gain.

In many translations of the Bible, the word "jewels" is translated as "rubies." To study for the original sermon that was the inspiration for this book, I did some research into rubies and found the following[2]:

- The ruby is a pink to blood-red gemstone which gets its red color because it contains the element chromium.

- Chromium is an element highly resistant to corrosion and is hard in its nature; in fact, on the sale of determining a stone's natural hardness, a ruby receives a 9.0, second only to mossianite and diamonds.

- A ruby is considered one of the four precious stones (rubies, emeralds, sapphires, and diamonds).

- All natural rubies have imperfections in them and their imperfections are what separate them from fake stones.

- All rubies must be treated (polished).

- Rubies are difficult to find. They are only mined in certain countries of the world.

Therefore, the reason women are compared to this

precious gem is most important and most relevant. The Proverbs 31 woman doesn't rust easily (deteriorate, fall into nothing) and remains firm and unmovable, no matter how much pressure is applied to her. Her imperfections are what separate her from imposters, and her power is made perfect in weakness. She isn't quite like anybody else, unique and valuable. She is polished by God, and hard to find, because she is the greatest blessing someone can find this side of heaven.

In keeping with being so important, it is relevant that the Proverbs 31 woman has a husband who trusts her. Much as we spoke of in our study of the Song of Solomon, our partners should recognize our worth. In Proverbs 31, such is reiterated in a practical sense. She is worthy of his confidence, and he is humbled before her and his accomplishments. This means she is fully capable of making her own decisions, she doesn't go running to her partner with every little thing, and she knows what qualifies as a decision to be discussed and one that does not.

A woman who brings good, and not evil

Proverbs 31:12:

She brings him good, not harm,
  all the days of her life.

If we are blessed women, we need to be women who have enough discernment to navigate between good and bad decisions. If we want to be trusted, we need to make ourselves trustworthy, and that means making the effort to bring good, rather than evil. We need to know the importance of being called to bring good and not evil into our lives and the lives of others and recognize that so many things could be different if we would exercise right discernment.

I've often described the gift of discernment as the "gift of knowing better." That's kind of a simplistic way of explaining the spiritual gift of discernment, but I think it's good to recognize discernment is not just a spiritual gift for use in specifically "spiritual designated" situations. Discernment also has an everyday life application, and the way it applies in everyday life is very similar to how I describe it in spiritual application. When we talk about being discerning, we are talking about having the ability to read a situation and make decisions based on the information presented. Sometimes we can think we are being a blessing or doing something good when what we are doing is enabling someone or bringing more difficulty to a situation. The difference is the result. We can't give everyone everything they always want, and what some people want is just not good for them, for us, or for the future. This is true with family, it is true with ministry, and it is true with life, in general.

On another note, we also need to recognize that when it comes to our relationships, we need to be a blessing to those we are involved with, especially those we are intimately involved with. This doesn't mean doing everything they want all the time, nor does it mean being a floormat for a mate. (Our lives should never entirely revolve around someone else.) It does mean that if we are in a godly relationship where we are treated well and God blesses us through our mate, we don't bring public (or private) disgrace to the one we love. We should pray for our mates, and ask God to intervene on their behalf, helping them to be successful.

Acts 18:24-26:

Meanwhile a Jew named Apollos, a native of Alexandria, came to Ephesus. He was a learned man, with a thorough knowledge of the Scriptures. He had been instructed in the way of the Lord, and he spoke with great fervor and taught about Jesus accurately, though he knew only the baptism of John. He began to speak boldly in the synagogue. When Priscilla and Aquilla heard him, they invited him to their home and explained to him the way of God more adequately.

An example of a Bible woman who brought good, and not evil, was Priscilla. She knew who she was in Christ, she knew her calling, she had her own ministerial identity and worked in blessing, and she was someone who sought to bring her mate good and not evil, all the days of her life. Priscilla and Aquilla worked together in ministry, and that means it was all the more important for her to be someone that inspired confidence. Nobody told her to be quiet, nobody shamed her, and nobody told her to take a back seat to her husband. She was a woman of complete confidence, one who was trustworthy, and one blessed to offer a balance as part of a team for God.

Productive, enterprising, empowered

Proverbs 31:13-20:

She selects wool and flax
  and works with eager hands.
She is like the merchant ships,
  bringing her food from afar.
She gets up while it is still night;
  she provides food for her family
  and portions for her female servants.
She considers a field and buys it;
  out of her earnings she plants a vineyard.
She sets about her work vigorously;
  her arms are strong for her tasks.
She sees that her trading is profitable,
  and her lamp does not go out at night.
In her hand she holds the distaff
  and grasps the spindle with her fingers.
She opens her arms to the poor
  and extends her hands to the needy.

If there is one thing that always irritates me, it is a lazy Christian. It doesn't matter to me what gender a lazy individual might be. "Lazy" and "Christian" just don't seem to go together to me. If we are Christians, we should be productive, and we should do things that make a difference in the world around us. This doesn't mean we can't have periods of rest or that sometimes we need to practice essential self-care, but that as people, we should aspire to accomplish things in our lives and utilize our time wisely.

A Proverbs 31 woman is not afraid to work. Before I get into discussion about this, I want to say that I believe all work is honorable before God, and it doesn't matter what form it takes. While there are many who think women shouldn't work, but instead take care of kids or family members, they are overlooking the fact that taking care of kids and family members and a household is work. Such is an important contribution in the life of a family. I don't believe, however, this is what women have to do in order to be productive. I take issue with people who say women only have a sphere that relates to household matters and who put women in the bind of feeling torn between work, helping to contribute to the funding of their household, and provide for their families. It also makes single parenting agonizing for women. Despite the circumstances that create single parenthood, the reality exists that single mothers do not have the option to stay home and parent their children full-time. I believe there are many different circumstances which arise for families, and wives and mothers must consider what is best for them at that point in time and do just that, rather than what someone else deems right.

This means: ladies, if you want to have a job, if you have a career that is important to you, if you work and you love it, or if you are at home with your kids, it's all right. There is no wrong way to be productive, if what you do is being productive and you do it unto the Lord. The same God Who created motherhood also created business, finance, education, medicine, and every other aspect of the working world. He doesn't just make mothers. He also makes doctors, lawyers, teachers, bankers, saleswomen, chefs, housekeepers, government officials, and every other type of job imaginable. No matter where you find your best fit, you're serving, in some capacity, unto the Lord.

Work, in whatever form it takes, teaches us about the world around us and that being productive is a way to engage others. Kids today tend to think the entire world revolves around them, and it's important they learn that sometimes mom is busy, and things have to wait, or that things are done and they come at a cost. It's also important to see teamwork, things require more than one person to be accomplished, and life moves much better as we work together rather than working separately. Whether a mom stays home or works, there is no excuse for treating her like a maid. Everyone contributes to the household in some form, and that includes helping, chores, and various responsibilities.

Being a blessed woman means we should be eager to do what we are called to do. We might get tired of it at times and even bored, but we should be competent in our business and bear fruit as we go along. Work is about more than compensation; it is also about taking pride in what we do well and in doing all things well.

We should also be women who embrace the principle of generosity. From what we have, we help to provide for our families. We come prepared, cautious, aware, and watchful of what is around us, whether it's in the bank, in the form of bills, outgoing flow, incoming money, and discipline over spending. From this, we have enough money to give to church, bless other people, and help those who are in need.

Along with diligence, we need to be women who finish what we start. Over my many years in ministry, I can't count the number of women I have worked with who start projects and never finish them. They want to do things, they enjoy things, they might even like the idea of something, but they don't discipline themselves to see it through. When the work is too much or the experience takes too long, they give up. In some instances, they give up because the task was too monumental for them to take on in the first place. If we are women who are honorable, that means we finish what we start. We don't take on things we shouldn't, and we consider our projects before we start them. If something is too big right now, we either find a way to downsize it, or we find a new project for the vision we can handle. We don't take on what we can handle and we discern, in advance, what will bless and what will burn. Obviously, we don't always do this a

BLESSED THOUGHTS:

A woman in God's work is never done

So often we've heard the words, "A woman's work is never done" to describe the business of a woman's life. I can testify I feel many days as if my work is never done. Sometimes the distribution of things seems so uneven, and life feels so stressful, I wonder what it would be like to just sit back and have nothing to do.

What I realize these days - now more than I ever have before - is that our work as women of God is never done. It will never be done until the time when Jesus returns. There are so many lives for us to touch, impact, help, and work to heal. There are so many ways for us to impact and affect those lives...and it makes me stand back and think to myself, I can't do this all by myself!

I'm correct in that thought. I can't do it all by myself. I don't have the resources or the physical capability. But I can do it with everyone else. As we work together to make a difference, we stop dividing ourselves into this cause and that cause. God has called us to stand with the hurting, support the strong, proclaim the Word, and bring about change wherever we go. Our job doesn't begin and end in the pulpit. While that's a part of it, we can all do something to make someone else's life better in a tangible way. We can reach out and listen. We can offer what we do have and use our gifts and calling for God's purpose. Most importantly, we can support one another. As we are all one body, everything every one of us is doing affects us all. Even though God may not tell us to do the same exact thing as another, we can always reach out and love our fellow workers in the harvest. This is especially important as women of the Gospel. So many are against us; so we all need to be for one another.

Yes, it's true...a woman in God's work is never done.

hundred percent, but we can do it enough to learn what's for us in any given situation.

No fear lives here

Proverbs 31:21-25:

When it snows, she has no fear for her household;
  for all of them are clothed in scarlet.
She makes coverings for her bed;
  she is clothed in fine linen and purple.
Her husband is respected at the city gate,
  where he takes his seat among the elders of the land.
She makes linen garments and sells them,
  and supplies the merchants with sashes.
She is clothed with strength and dignity;
  she can laugh at the days to come.

We talk a lot against fear in church, but we often use fear to entertain and intimidate from the pulpit. Whether we are talking about the end of the world, fear over changing society, political fears, world events, or a change in culture, we are quick to use fear to make sure that others respond quickly to buy whatever we're selling.

Thus, I think our "no fear" message has a few holes in it. It isn't a wonder to me that Christian women are often quite fearful: fearful about not getting married, about their spouses, about being the right kind of woman, for their children, if they are doing the wrong thing or living the wrong kind of way, and so on and so forth. What I see in Proverbs 31 is a clear advisement that if we prepare ourselves, we won't encounter fear like we often do. We shouldn't be standing on such a state of constant fear and worry, because God has told us our confidence is in Him. Thus, if our confidence is in Him, we must trust Him to bring things to pass in due season and be diligent in the meantime.

There is an African Proverb: "While you pray, move your feet." This doesn't mean dance while you pray, it means do something while you wait on God to answer your prayer. Things that surprise us often shouldn't, and they surprise us because we aren't diligent and persistent in doing the things that are right, all along.

If we are prepared and expecting things such as seasons to change (both spiritual and natural), we are doing our best to provide where we can and create beautiful places of comfort and safety. If we are doing what we can to be productive, we should have no reason to fear. Rather, we should laugh at the days to come because we can anticipate them with excitement and joy. If we attend to our business, we can trust that God will attend to ours.

Balancing home and work

Proverbs 31:26-27:

*She speaks with wisdom,
  and faithful instruction is on her tongue.
She watches over the affairs of her household
  and does not eat the bread of idleness.*

There is a great blessing in being wise. One of the things people tell me they like most about my mom is her extensive wisdom. Even though my mom is not a big church leader like some others she might encounter, her wisdom is heard by great and small alike and embraced by many. Wisdom speaks; it reaches; it touches. It gives powerful insight for now, as well as what is next.

In wisdom, we need to speak when it's time to speak. There is nothing about the Proverbs 31 woman that is passive, and that means we shouldn't approach life with a passive spirit. Being passive, taking second best all the time, or always making sure that others speak, and you don't isn't the spirit of excellence; it is fear and intimidation. As doers, we are also speakers, and we are people confident in the voice and perspective God has given to us.

Rise up and call her blessed

Proverbs 31:28-31:

*Her children arise and call her blessed;
  her husband also, and he praises her:
"Many women do noble things,
  but you surpass them all."
Charm is deceptive, and beauty is fleeting;*

but a woman who fears the LORD is to be praised.
Honor her for all that her hands have done,
* and let her works bring her praise at the city gate.*

It disturbs me deeply when we try to downplay the influence and purpose of women in life. It seems to me that we are so busy trying to look so "fair" and "equitable" all the time that we are afraid to say something that might raise a woman up and help her to feel confident in herself and in her abilities. We're afraid that if we say too much that is positive for her, we'll offend her children, or a man, or society at large, or advocate values that we aren't supposed to advocate in church. The truth is that there is no more family-positive message I can think of than to raise up a woman who is doing what God would have her to do and let her know that she can do exactly what she is appointed to do.

We, as women, often have very full plates. We work in some capacity, we handle our families (whether nuclear or extended), we maintain church memberships or lead ministries, and we care for our households. The Proverbs 31 woman did too, which is why she is a reflection of every single one of us. She went from work to home, making decisions, encountering children and family, and balancing life and relationship with her husband. She knew how to be diligent and accountable and knew that what she did was honorable.

If you are doing what you know you should be doing and are doing your very best (even if what you are doing right now is just temporary), then you need to hear your children, your family, your spouse, and your heavenly Father call you blessed. You need to know that you are doing your best, and it really is good enough. She is worthy of her reward, because no matter how much money we might spend on vanity, eventually our looks will fade...but good, diligent, and awesome is forever.

God calls us to be more than skin-deep vain, and there is more than one way to be barely skin-deep. Whether it's being wrapped up in appearances, being fake and in denial, being dishonest, or just being two-faced, none of these things lead to praiseworthy conduct. The fruit of our hands speak for themselves and praise us for what we do that is right and amazing. Let our fruit speak louder than surface behavior, and instead of playing a part, let's be a part of the Kingdom as God has called us to be.

As women, let's be more than what the world tells us to be, and more than a laundry list of to-dos and to-don'ts. Let's be rubies, women of excellence and rare values, just doing and being what God has created us to be.

Reflections

- What kind of teaching have you heard about the Proverbs 31 woman?

- When you hear about the Proverbs 31 woman, how does it make you feel?

- How can you relate to the woman's life in Proverbs 31 and what we know of it?

CHAPTER SEVEN

The Barren Woman
- Blessed With Emptiness -

"SING, BARREN WOMAN, YOU WHO NEVER BORE A CHILD; BURST INTO SONG, SHOUT FOR JOY, YOU WHO WERE NEVER IN LABOR; BECAUSE MORE ARE THE CHILDREN OF THE DESOLATE WOMAN THAN OF HER WHO HAS A HUSBAND," SAYS THE LORD.
(ISAIAH 54:1)

Of all the "blessed" women I studied for the original sermon this book stems from, I found the barren woman to be the most interesting. Calling this woman "blessed" was a promise that totally defied anything and everything that ancient culture assigned to women, and even that it assigns to women right down to the present day. Leave it to God to do something totally outrageous and unconventional, just like that! In cultures that treated procreation as if it was the exclusive ticket to eternity, God declared the woman who had no children – who was unable to procreate – as blessed.

Having said that, we need to take a long look at this blessing, because it is relevant and special in a different way. It speaks to us about making room for differences and different people, those who have a different walk in life and a different experience when it comes to matters such as family, children, and marriage. There is still a stigma that we need to follow a certain path through life: marriage, kids, the house with the white-picket fence, the minivan, the birthdays and graduations, and then the grandkids. There is nothing wrong with wanting this in your life or having it. If it's what you seek, then it's what you should have. But I think there is a part of many people that are either very uncomfortable with those who make choices or are thrust into other choices that are outside of the so-called "norm." It's not because they are bad, but because these situations cause people to be different and look at what they have and where they are in a different way.

We need people like this in our world. Sometimes we get so preoccupied with family and trying to attract families to church, we give the message that traditional family is all that's welcome in a ministry setting. We forget about those who might feel marginalized or not accepted because their situations are different. It reminds us that the Kingdom, the church, the realm of God is big enough for all of us, different from what might be most socially accepted, proving to us that God's blessings are beyond what everyone might want, think, or imagine in comfortable places.

Women in the time of the barren woman

There are barren women all throughout the Bible, all of whom lived in different times and eras. Some of these women included Sarah, Hannah, Elizabeth, Michal, Manoah's wife (Samson's mother), Anna, Dorcas (Tabitha), Huldah, Vashti, Esther, Jehosheba, Martha, Joanna, Miriam, and Priscilla. While some of these women were temporarily barren (they did go on to have children), some of the women mentioned here had no recorded children in their Biblical accounts. This means that infertility has been a long-standing issue in society, and there have been different feelings in response to it, depending upon the woman involved and the times in which she lived.

For example, barrenness was a severe stigma for

Hannah, who wrestled with feelings of inferiority because she was barren (and we shall talk about her a little later). Priscilla and Joanna, both New Testament figures who were busy with ministry, don't appear to have struggled with infertility in the same way that Hannah did. This doesn't mean they didn't experience her frustration or feelings, but something else became more important in their lives which changed their perception of the struggle. In the overall sense of their cultures, not having children was regarded as a failure of the woman, because marriage was seen as a primary vehicle for procreation. Having heirs, especially male heirs, was a big deal. It ensured property remained in families and that family names continued. That means women were expected to have children, and if a couple was unable to have children, the woman got the blame.

Galatians 4:27:

[For] It is written in the Scriptures: "Be happy [Rejoice], barren one [Jerusalem]. You are like a woman who never gave birth to children. Start singing [Burst out] and shout for joy [cry out]. You never felt the pain of giving birth [or went into labor], but you who are childless [desolate; or deserted] will have more children than the woman who has a husband [Is. 54:1]." (EXB)

Even now, there is a certain societal stigma around women who do not have children, for one reason or another. I have experienced this firsthand in my own life, my testimony of which I will give in the next section of this chapter. It's a reality that we live with as women: we are told we have so much time to have children, we are encouraged to pursue it, and it is the big question that surrounds our lives. It is as if nothing is considered higher, more important, or more relevant in the life of a woman. If she feels that there is something else for her to do or has a different calling, she might encounter shame, name-calling, criticism, or attack of character. Being what is classified as "barren," or childless, is still regarded in a negative light, especially for women.

My story as the "barren woman"

Isaiah 41:22-23:

This is what the Lord GOD says:
"See, I will lift My hand to signal [to] the nations;
 I will raise My banner for all the people to see.
Then they will bring your sons back to you in their arms
 [bosom; lap],
 and they will carry your daughters on their shoulders
[Jews returning from exile are pictured as children
 returning to their parents].
Kings will teach your children [be guardians/foster
 parents],
 and daughters of kings [princesses; or queens] will
 take care of them.
They will bow down before you with their faces to the
 ground
 and kiss the dirt [lick the dust] at your feet.
Then you will know I am the LORD.
 Anyone who trusts in [hopes in; waits on] Me will not
be disappointed [or ashamed]." (EXB)

When I first wrote this book, I offered some basic information about my own journey as the "barren woman." For the sake of privacy, I didn't disclose as many details as I could have, opting instead to try and present an "empowered" view of the barren woman. At this time, I recognize empowerment comes in many more forms than I might have conveyed, and it's important to tell the whole of a story rather than omitting parts (at least as pertains to what's relevant).

There isn't room to tell my entire testimony here, save the aspects that are relevant to our topic. As the "barren woman" myself, I've known for quite some time, probably most of my life, that I would be childless, at least for most of it. I remember being a young child and telling adults I was never going to have any children. The adults in my life either laughed or blew me off, telling me, "You'll change your mind!" If there was one thing I hated as a rather intense child, it was when people didn't take me seriously. Being taken seriously has always been important to me, and treating me as if what I said had no relevance because it was assumed my views would change was to blow off all the reasons I didn't want children. Nobody ever asked me why I didn't want to have children or what my other goals were. They just assumed, as they do with all children, that my ideas would change when I was "mature."

As an adult, I would be remiss if I didn't admit that my first marriage wasn't stable enough to handle our relationship, let alone a whole other being. My late husband stated repeatedly he wanted a "motorcycle and a boat," and there wasn't room for any children financially. The most it came up was to say if I wanted to have a baby, he would go along with it, but I would bear the full responsibility for a child's care. That was enough for me to continue in my stance against having children. I wanted to focus on my career in ministry, and being a mother without spousal assistance would render ministry impossible.

This didn't stop me from having two miscarriages that were the result of unplanned pregnancies. Sometimes we can use everything we are supposed to and do everything we are supposed to, and accidents happen anyway. The miscarriages were so early, I didn't know I was pregnant until the "chemical pregnancy" (as it is called) terminated itself. I remember being upset, not that I had miscarried, but that I would have been faced with decisions if I hadn't. There would have been no way I could have faced a pregnancy and parenthood if nature hadn't made the decision for me.

I've always been fine not having any biological kids. There isn't a lot of respect for that in ministry, however. It was expected women in my age group should desire to have children and be busy with that for many years to avoid competing with older women who approached ministry as a second career. I found myself in the middle of that competition, and those who encouraged me to do things outside of ministry did so with selfish ambition. If I was preoccupied with babies, young children, and family life, I would have been otherwise occupied and not present as competition for these older female ministers.

I suspect had I followed a more "normal" course of life in the eyes of many of my female colleagues, I wouldn't have been as ostracized as I was. They wouldn't have seen me as a threat and would have had the opportunity to be more mentors (even though I wouldn't have asked for their advice). I wrestled deeply with the issue of feeling out of place for a long time, especially as the negative responses came in from others. When you don't have children, no one assumes maybe your desire to be childless is heaven-sent, or perhaps you're unable to have them, or maybe your marriage can't withstand them. The fact you don't have them is judged, and people assume you're doing so to deliberately not fit in with societal norms.

It tickles me to think that not having children follows course with relationship anarchy. With the number of children born under dire or unfair circumstances or who are unwanted and unloved, you would think being responsible to such a decision would be respected, but that's not what happened to me, at all. I found the opposite. I have had people tell me I didn't have a nurturing spirit, which was a requirement for being a Christian woman. I had someone outright tell me they thought it was me that didn't want children and not God, and that I needed to "adjust" myself and my thinking. I've had people try to "pray" me into childbirth, try to speak children over me, and have people pray that my will would change. I dealt with people who tried to get me to babysit or try to get me to bring children into my life, telling me it would fix how I felt.

Dealing with this for so many years played games with my mind, to the point where it made me feel like I was a problem. I reached a place of clarity in realizing these aren't decisions others can make for us. I wasn't sitting around, judging these other women for how they raised their children (even though there might have been good reason to do so). Some of the pushiest women had children addicted to drugs, in prison, in and out of destructive relationships, and unable to hold down employment. They were busy judging me to cover up their own parenting inadequacies, hoping if I continued the trend, it might take the heat off them. Yet it doesn't change that in their own attempts to puff themselves up, they tried to tear me down.

In hindsight, I support the decision I made to remain childless in my first marriage. I was the one who would have to live with the consequences of that decision, and I made the right choice for myself and my very complicated marriage.

After my first husband died, I didn't expect to remarry. Even though I was a young widow (I was 37 when he died), I figured marriage and family was behind me. I felt I missed out on possibly good experiences in marriage, but I wasn't sure what was ahead for me. I assumed I'd probably remain single — and childless — for the rest of my life. I embraced the idea of spiritual motherhood — of spiritually parenting individuals abandoned by their families and leading my congregation well — not as a substitution, but as a sincere calling, recognizing this is part of why I'm at this point in my life.

We speak of God surprises often. Well, my second husband is one of those surprises. As of the revision of this book we haven't been married long, but we have discussed the possibility of family. Given age and reproductive challenges, it's possible biological parenthood won't be for us. Either way, we recognize the importance of adoption, especially for children who aren't as easy to place and need families. A specific course isn't clear right now, but no matter what happens, we are grateful to have each other and we are enjoying our period of barrenness, as I have throughout my entire life.

No matter what happens in my situation, I'm comfortable being the "barren woman." My life has empty places that are filled by spiritual pursuits and projects. I enjoy being a "spiritual mom." I'm blessed to be a wife, enjoying her new marriage. It's awesome to write books, see tasks come to fruition, and to be focused on Kingdom things. I am excited to know — and walk in —

the special blessing God has for me. It empowers me and is for me. It is different from a blessing that someone else might have, but it is a part of the calling that makes me who I am.

The stereotype of barrenness

I'm not here to put down women who choose to have children or who want to have them. Infertility can be a terribly painful experience. As we go through this chapter, you will find the true definition of barrenness is not necessarily what we always think it is. In the same vein, however, so many messages geared for women are all about children and family. One can easily get the message that this is all there is for women. In looking at the barren woman, we realize the Bible offers praise and encouragement for situations that don't fall into comfortable norms. We find extensive praise for women who are single and women who are without children as well as praise and admiration for the woman who is married and has children. Here we are looking at an unconventional woman, one who is different and who has a different experience, and that experience and blessing needs to be embraced, because it is one we will all experience at some point in time.

Even though we don't like to admit it, and as my own testimony confirms, there is a very intense cultural bias (translated to a Christian bias by extension) in favor of having children and raising families present in most, if not all, cultures in the world.

I Samuel 1:1-8:

There was a certain man from Ramathaim, a Zuphite from the hill country of Ephraim, whose name was Elkanah son of Jeroham, the son of Elihu, the son of Tohu, the son of Zuph, an Ephraimite. He had two wives; one was called Hannah and the other Peninnah. Peninnah had children, but Hannah had none.

Year after year this man went up from his town to worship

and sacrifice to the LORD Almighty at Shiloh, where Hophni and Phineas, the two sons of Eli, were priests of the LORD. Whenever the day came for Elkanah to sacrifice, he would give portions of the meat to his wife Peninnah and to all her sons and daughters. But to Hannah he gave a double portion because he loved her, and the LORD had closed her womb. Because the LORD had closed Hannah's womb, her rival kept provoking her in order to irritate her. This went on year after year. Whenever Hannah went up to the house of the LORD, her rival provoked her till she wept and would not eat. Her husband Elkanah would say to her, "Hannah, why are you weeping? Why don't you eat? Why are you downhearted? Don't I mean more to you than ten sons?"

The story of Hannah and her intense feelings about having a baby reflects typical attitudes about childbearing in Bible times. She saw herself as unworthy and unvalued because she was unable to have children. This continues to be part of our world today. Now we know Hannah had a greater vision and the child she was to have would be very special. Hannah didn't have this knowledge yet. Her deep feelings of inferiority compared to Peninnah and other women who had children was very, very cultural and hurtful to her.

Each nation desires to be prosperous, large, and be able to withstand a large population. Militaries need bodies, and military bodies are selected from the largest possible pool of eligible candidates. In more modern times, we might say we need more bodies to boost the Social Security program, or the fear that populations might not have enough younger bodies to care for aging ones. The obvious result is a strong contempt for people who don't have children. Here we find the byproduct: the woman's expectation to have children. While most societies don't mandate women have a certain number of children, it is implied by expectation and social dialogue that each woman will have at least one child. In keeping with social expectation, there remain countries in the world where women can be divorced, put away, or even abused for not bearing children within marriage.

This does not count the number of marriages which end or remain dissatisfied or stressed because they cannot have children and want to do so out of their own desire.

What is barrenness?

Merriam-Wesbster's Online Dictionary defines "barrenness" as:

1 : not reproducing: as *a*: incapable of producing offspring –used especially of females or matings *b*: not yet or not recently pregnant *c*: habitually failing to fruit
2: not productive: as *a*: producing little or no vegetation: desolate *<barren deserts> b*: producing inferior crops *<barren soil> c*: unproductive of results or gain: fruitless *<a barren scheme>*
3: devoid, lacking –used with *of <barren of excitement>*
4: lacking interest or charm *<a barren routine>*
5: lacking inspiration or ideas *<a barren mind>*[3]

Even the dictionary is inconsistent in its definition of "barrenness." The basic definition of barrenness is not reproducing, but there are two different ways people can be barren. There is biological barrenness, which is caused by either a man or woman (or sometimes even a combination of the two) and some sort of genetic or biological barrier to reproduction (i.e., the couple is unable to conceive or carry to the point where the baby is born). The other type of barrenness is intentional: when a woman or a man (and preferably the couple agrees), having knowledge and understanding of reproduction and how to prevent it (whether permanently or temporarily), take measures to avoid conception through various means of birth control or abstinence.

Different people feel different ways about barrenness. Some people are very grieved about the situation. It truly pains them in their souls, such as was Hannah's experience. Some people seek methods to overcome barrenness, such as fertility treatments, surrogacy, or even adoption. But there are plenty who feel like I do and enjoy and embrace life without children. For such as these, they celebrate barrenness.

In the continued definition, barrenness is also associated with being unfruitful, unproductive, and empty. As a result, it is worth a look at how much we associate with and attach to fertility in our culture. We regard those without children just like the definition: empty, fruitless, unproductive, and as a wasteland.

Judges 13:2-3:

There was a man named Manoah from the tribe of Dan, who lived in the city of Zorah [fifteen miles west of Jerusalem; v. 25]. He had a wife, but she [was barren/infertile and] could not have children [a cause of both sadness and shame; Gen. 11:30; 29:31]. The angel [messenger] of the Lord [angelic spokesperson for God, sometimes identified with the Lord Himself; 2:1; 6:11; Gen. 16:7; Ex. 14:19; 23:20] appeared to Manoah's wife and said, "You [Look/Behold, you are barren and] have not been able to have children, but you will become pregnant [conceive] and give birth to a son. (EXB)

Whether or not a woman is comfortable with her barrenness, she pays a great stigma for being barren within her culture. The constant evaluation of a woman as to whether she has children is a great pain that women, both comfortable with barrenness and uncomfortable with it, pay in the cultures in which they live. The truth, however, is that if we truly look at the definition, every woman is "barren" at some point in their lives, or another. All of us have periods of time when we are not reproducing. For example, women who have gone through menopause are "barren" at that point in their lives. Women who aren't ready to have children yet are also classified as "barren," and women who have had children in the past and are now past the point of having more children are, according to the definition, also "barren."

Being barren is actually very special, because it is something all women go through at some point in time. It means that there is room in your life to be open to something else, to something new and different.

Can we have it all?

I think the question of barrenness and the way it is often approached comes down to seriously answering the question, "Can we have it all?" We like to always have all the options open and available to us. Behind this, I think it's because we don't want to take anything off the table in case we dislike the choice we made. We want to have everything: the great looking house, the big cars, the white picket fence, the two-and-a-half attractive and obedient kids, the home-cooked meals, the competent and wealthy spouse, and we also now want the successful career and divine calling from God, all to be pursued when we are ready and when we think the timing is best.

Luke 10:42:

"There's only one thing you need. Mary has made the right choice, and that one thing will not be taken away from her." (GW)

As much as we might like to have all these options available to us at once, it's not realistic to think we can pursue all these things and pursue them well at the same time. Life demands our choices. If we are to do things with wisdom and order, we recognize we can't do everything we want, all the time, at once. Making choices is God-given, because God gives us choices. But choosing one thing means we do not have all the other options at our disposal anymore. All choices have consequences and benefits with them, and we must recognize that in a world that doesn't like to close doors, in closing one door we open up the door for God to do something else new and different in our lives.

For example: people speak of being a parent as a great blessing in their lives, a blessing with seemingly immediate results and that may be what brings them a blessing about it. They get to watch their children grow and develop, and they are excited about that process. In choosing that blessing, they give up a lot of other things: sleeping late on the weekends, the freedom to come and go as they please, being able to spend money the way they always desire, having endless free time, quiet, privacy, and an adult social life. To get a blessing in one form, there are other blessings they must give up in the process.

The divine hand of God extends to all of us, and there is blessing present no matter where we are at in our lives. Just as there is a blessing in having children, there is also a blessing in barrenness. It opens the door for God to work something spiritual in our lives that we can't have when we are busy being blessed in different ways, by different things.

The reality is that our lives change. With the changes in our lives come different choices, and all of us are faced with barrenness by situational biology or some choice in our lives. Here, a woman is in a position to welcome in a new thing of God, because her life is not already overly full of blessings she already has.

Room to birth in the spiritual

Perhaps the greatest thing we must realize in this teaching about barrenness is that societal stigma against women who are barren is a principle of emphasizing natural birth over spiritual birth. Being able to procreate physically is a part of the natural realm and natural order: it is how most are built and wired in our bodies, and procreation is something every life form in natural order can do, unless there is some sort of biological problem. Frogs can have tadpoles, germs can multiply, and everything under the sun has a means to reproduce after its own kind. For much of the plant and animal kingdom, living, reproducing, and surviving until death is about all they accomplish in their lives. Once they are gone, most of the animal kingdom does not even realize a specific, individual creature was there. We, being in the image and likeness of God, however, means we are here to do more than just live, reproduce, and die. Our life pursuit is more than procreation. Our design is higher, different, and this incessant push for procreation in the natural distracts from the spiritual development that so many of us need in our lives.

This means that while there is nothing wrong with having natural children, having many children for no other reason but to have many children is not a spiritual pursuit. In the Scriptures. The children who were the biggest blessing to their parents were spiritually minded, not those who came into the world and then brought them disgrace. Even when women have children, they must teach their children the virtues of spiritual things. That starts with seeking spiritual things for herself. It is for these purposes that makes Jesus' words to the women about barrenness most poignant in a deeper way.

Luke 23:27-31:

A large number of people followed Him, including women who mourned and wailed for Him. Jesus turned and said to them, "Daughters of Jerusalem, do not weep for Me; weep for yourselves and for your children. For the time will come when you will say, 'Blessed are the childless women, the wombs that never bore and the breasts that never nursed!' Then

"they will say to the mountains, "Fall on us!"
  and to the hills, "Cover us!"

For if men do these things when the tree is green, what will happen when it is dry?"

Even on His way to the cross, Jesus provided words encouraging deeper faith and spiritual depth within His followers. It also tells us women especially need to make room for God to birth in their lives. When the entire world is falling apart, we women need to be spiritual enough to empty ourselves of this world. Sometimes we are so busy being full − full of responsibilities, full of duties, full of work, and full of the cares of life − that we don't have room for

BLESSED THOUGHTS:

Spiritual birth for women

Several years ago, I was present in a conference where the conference host continually made reference to the fact that it "takes a man and a woman to create life." It was ultimately used against women to state that women in ministry who weren't married were "setting themselves up for trouble and failure." Not only did this single statement totally discredit the awesome and incredible work of God's single women throughout history (including those in the Bible, such as the four daughters of Philip in Acts 21:9), it yet again reduced the church to its two-fold stereotype: both sexism and single-minded procreation. In his words were the timeless message that women need men, women can't be complete without men - and this was most definitely a stab on women as he made no statements on the warnings against single men in ministry. Even though we all know that there are plenty of single male preachers and ministers who sleep around, that seems to go without mention when there's a single woman in the room who has overcome the stereotype that she "needs" a man. It also pushes women to get married despite what God may say to them. Out of fear their ministries will be hampered or out of some warped concept of order, women find themselves distracted from the things of God. This also leaves her vulnerable to have her ministry vision stolen, hijacked, or compromised by a prowling man who seeks a woman vulnerable enough to manipulate and abuse in the spiritual and emotional realms.

What is most relevant, however, is the elevation of the natural level to that of the supernatural. While I am certainly not denouncing family life or the desire to have a family, be married, or have children, we seem to exclude the idea that women can have their own ministries, relationships with God, and purposes in life aside from men. The more I realized what was happening in this message, the more upset I became. I recognized the sting of patriarchy alive and well, multiplying its seeds. On the surface, it sounds great and uniting. In reality, it's meant to keep men in control of women. Not only is this mentality not of God, it is the opposite of God, as a perpetual notion of the world. If we acknowledge God as counter-culture, we cannot embrace such a sexist attitude because it is dominated by worldly thinking. As we change, we become more aware of these ideas, and rather than embrace them, we are called to develop a deeper spiritual understanding. One of the most basic ways we do this is by recognizing the way spirit operates versus the progression of natural order.

The spiritual realm does not operate by the laws of the present natural order. Such an example of this is in the arena of procreation. Frogs and toads can reproduce according to natural order, but they do not have the ability to multiply and generate spiritual children. The same is true for human beings, no matter how much we may dislike hearing this. Just because people have large families with the ability to procreate does not mean the result of such efforts is spiritual in nature. Parenting is not a spiritual venture in the natural realm; it is a natural order. This does not mean parents cannot train up children in spiritual matters, but it does mean that in and of itself, parenting is not of the spiritual realm. In the natural realm, both a male and female are required for reproduction. This, however, does not translate to being true in the spirit realm - and therefore, we cannot pin the requirements of natural reproduction on that of spiritual reproduction. We can see from the examples of spiritual progenitors the truth in this matter: Jesus was begotten of the Father with no man in the picture (John 1:1), God creates spiritual children by His Spirit without the requirement of their spiritual regeneration in opposite-sex pairs (Romans 8:14), and Jesus' ability to multiply His disciples without Jesus Himself being married or without the procreative will of a couple (John 1:12). The same is true for women in terms of spiritual birth. In the example I will show below, the example of spiritual birth in women without a man is in some ways extraordinarily powerful. It is empowering for us, as women, to recognize that we can bring forth spiritual life and power no matter our station in life, whether our husbands, fathers, or boyfriends are on board; and that we can stand spiritually independent without being in some sort of order/authority violation.

All the way back in Genesis 3:15, we find a unique prophecy:

"And I will put enmity between you and the woman, and between your offspring and hers; He will crush your head, and you will strike his heel."

Way back in the garden, God spoke of the power of a supernatural birth which would defy natural order. It is impossible for a woman to have "offspring" or 'seed," as it is translated in the King James Version. For procreation to occur by natural order, "seed" is deposited by the man - a woman does not have her own "seed." Yet the Bible is clear in stating that a woman would bear offspring - it would not be the product of a man and a woman, but as far as the natural eye could see, it would be her seed. This birth would be supernatural, spiritual, and beyond anything that could be conceived by natural order. This prophecy as we know was fulfilled in Mary:

But the angel said to her, "Do not be afraid, Mary; you have found favor with God. You will conceive and give birth to a Son, and you are to call Him Jesus. He will be great and will be called the Son of the Most High. The Lord God will give Him the throne of His father David, and He will reign over jacob's descendants forever; His Kingdom will never end."

"How will this be," Mary asked the angel, "since I am a virgin?" The angel answered, "The Holy Spirit will come upon you, and the power of the Most High will overshadow you. So the Holy One to be born will be called the Son of God. Even Elizabeth your relative is going to have a child in her old age, and she who was said to be unable to conceive is in her sixth month. For no word from God will ever fail." (Luke 1:30-37)

For this great miracle to occur, it took Mary and the Holy Spirit. Joseph didn't have to be present, nor did he have to be consulted. He didn't have to like it, agree to it, or think another thing of it. All he had to do was cooperate with the great spiritual birth at work in Mary and not interfere in the process. He was also commanded to stay with Mary, no matter what the world might have thought. This was something spiritual! (This is a message for the men of spiritually birthing women - just cooperate and share in what God births through the woman in your life)

Even though we will never see another virgin birth this side of heaven, we too can recognize the process of spiritual birth within us. God is still working and birthing great things through the women who stand as warriors for Him in the Kingdom. For women to birth in the spiritual, it doesn't take a man. It doesn't take a husband. It doesn't require natural law or natural order. All it took for Mary to birth Jesus was the full indwelling of the Holy Spirit in this special way in her life.

For us, it is the same: to birth in the spiritual we need to accept the overshadowing of the Holy Spirit, His total indwelling, living in total obedience to God. Many of us claim to want great things, but we think we must obtain them by natural means. We can't compromise the spiritual with the natural. Just as Mary lived with challenges and complications from her choices, we too will face the same. Yet I doubt she ever regretted her decision to birth spiritually: Jesus lives forever. What we birth in the natural may die, but what we birth in the Spirit is eternal.

As we become a few of the world's many women who make natural sacrifices to birth in the spiritual, I pray we will never be caught up in false mindsets and open ourselves to true revelation of the Scriptures that will encourage our spiritual birth. No matter what may seem impossible in the natural, let us never forget the words of Mary in praise to God:

And Mary said: "My soul glorifies the Lord and my spirit rejoices in God my Savior, for He has been mindful of the humble state of His servant. From now on all generations will call me blessed, for the Mighty One has done great things for me – holy is His Name." (Luke 1:46-49)

the spiritual filling that comes from spiritual birth.

Is this passage of Scripture, quoted on the other page, a curse? Some do read it that way. They defend their views by making natural reproduction the highest life's purpose, over that of barrenness. I don't believe it is a curse. If there is a choice to be barren and it is a decision we can make for ourselves, then no, it is not a curse. What Jesus does is very counterculture in this singular passage of Scripture: He clarifies a woman's purpose is not just about childbearing – they have a greater purpose than just being used for reproduction. In a time that was to come, which we could parallel to be the "last days" (the time between the resurrection and when Jesus returns), people would honor the barren woman, not just because children behave in ways that are sometimes out of control, but also because of Joel 2:28-29's prophecy that women would receive the Spirit:

"And afterward,
I will pour out My Spirit on all people.
Your sons and daughters will prophesy,

*your old men will dream dreams,
your young men will see visions.
Even on My servants, both men and women,
I will pour out My Spirit in those days."* (GW)

The barren woman is ready to be spiritually filled to receive that Spirit. She finds blessing in that reception. We are blessed because our very lives prove that God has a purpose for women beyond the childbearing cultural demands of this world and it is a mighty and awesome journey.

The spiritual promise

Galatians 4:21-30:

Those who want to be controlled by Moses' laws should tell me something. Are you really listening to what Moses' Teachings say? Scripture says that Abraham had two sons, one by a woman who was a slave and the other by a free woman. Now, the son of the slave woman was conceived in a natural way, but the son of the free woman was conceived through a promise made to Abraham.

I'm going to use these historical events as an illustration. The women illustrate two arrangements. The one woman, Hagar, is the arrangement made on Mount Sinai. Her children are born into slavery. Hagar is Mount Sinai in Arabia. She is like Jerusalem today because she and her children are slaves. But the Jerusalem that is above is free, and she is our mother. Scripture says:

*"Rejoice, women who cannot get pregnant,
who cannot give birth to any children!
Break into shouting, those who feel no pains of childbirth!
Because the deserted woman will have more children
than the woman who has a husband."*

Now you, brothers and sisters, are children of the promise like Isaac.

Furthermore, at that time the son who was conceived in a natural way persecuted the son conceived in a spiritual way. That's exactly what's happening now. But what does Scripture say? "Get rid of the slave woman and her son, because the son of the slave woman must never share the inheritance with the son of the free woman." (GW)

We can see here, again, this promise that the barren woman – the spiritually open woman – bears because what is born is of the Spirit. As believers, we are all the children of God, spiritually mature heirs through our spiritual inheritance. We reap the spiritual because we received what was born in us spiritually. It was begotten of God, not by man or a human conception or birth. Therefore, we know, understand, and embrace the spiritual beyond the physical realm. We know so much more is out there for us. We might not perceive it all the time with our sight, but we are able to see it by our faith.

Jerusalem from above, the New Jerusalem, is described in this passage as being our true spiritual mother. It is where we come from and where we dwell as children of God, and our access to this does not come from a natural birth. We are children of the New Covenant and recognize that by the Spirit. In recognizing this spiritual power, we see that spiritual birth is always opposed to culture: God never does what people expect or does things in what may be perceived to be a socially acceptable manner.

That means He is calling and blessing an entire body of the female population that is currently socially unacceptable, in one form or another. All praise to the amazing God we serve, Who never does anything expected! Women all over the world are carrying something spiritual, rather than natural, at this moment. They are receiving the divine blessing from above, walking and standing upon spiritual realities we share with others as we remain present here on this earth. Even though it is a thing of heaven, we celebrate our experience of it, right now!

Physically barren, spiritually rich

John chapter 3 (the passage where Jesus speaks on the new birth) isn't a passage that most people are unfamiliar with. It is unfortunate, though, that we miss some key things when reading these passages. We tend to skip ideas because we read them through the lens of tradition or culture, rather than spiritual insight.

John 3:1-8:

Now there was a Pharisee, a man named Nicodemus who was a member of the Jewish ruling council. He came to Jesus at night and said, "Rabbi, we know that You are a teacher Who has come from God. For no one could perform the signs You are doing if God were not with Him."

Jesus replied, "Very truly I tell you, no one can see the Kingdom of God unless they are born again."

"How can someone be born when they are old?" Nicodemus asked. "Surely they cannot enter a second time into their mother's womb to be born!"

Jesus answered, "Very truly I tell you, no one can enter the Kingdom of God unless they are born of water and the Spirit. Flesh gives birth to flesh, but the Spirit gives birth to spirit. You should not be surprised at My saying, 'You must be born again.' The wind blows wherever it pleases. You hear its sound, but you cannot tell where it comes from or where it is going. So it is with everyone born of the Spirit."

The important "birth" which Jesus speaks of here comes not by woman, but by God. It is most key that Jesus clarifies flesh gives birth to flesh. We, as women, can have as many children as we like. By so doing, in this natural realm (without the Spirit) we will give birth to flesh, no matter how hard we try to give birth to something else. In the natural world, we cannot give birth to Spirit.

With those results, no matter how hard we try, every mother will battle in the flesh through with her children's disobedience. More solid, holy women have children who are totally rebellious, disobedient, and disrespectful to their mothers and their calling than we'd like to admit. Those wonderful Norman Rockwell painting-like visions of Christian motherhood don't always happen, and we need to stop wondering what these women have done wrong. Instead, we need to acknowledge those kids have been born in flesh, not Spirit. They too have choices and decisions to make and it's not necessarily their mother's fault, or their father's fault, or anyone's fault that these children follow the flesh rather than the Spirit.

This is why we are to be rich in the Spirit: the natural world disappoints us. As we grow in the Spirit, we must free ourselves of these hurts and disappointments, even if we hold onto them as our own. We need to move to a state of natural barrenness: where we stop trying to fill ourselves with natural order, so we can become spiritually filled.

When we are spiritually filled, we become pregnant with the promises of God. They are born in us, better than anything the natural world can offer. God is ready to bless His women, but we need to be emptied of the world so we can be filled with Him!

The more I go along in ministry, the more I am in awe of the Spirit and realizing the importance of what He wants to do as we empty ourselves. For so many years, I was preoccupied with so many natural things that I totally disregarded spiritual things. I would have easily traded spiritual things for natural things. Even though I wasn't full of natural children, I was full of concerns about money, prestige, moving up in the world, and I would have gladly traded the Spirit for any one of those things, as bad as I am sure such sounds. I have met so many women over the years who feel exactly the same way about one thing or another. They would sell their soul to have a baby in the natural world and ignore the great things they could have in the spiritual if they would stop seeking natural things. They would give up any spiritual purpose or destiny to find a husband or not have to cover the bills on their own anymore. They would do anything in this world to get a different job or a promotion. It sounds dangerous when we talk about it like this, but there are so many out there who feel the same way, for one thing or another, because they don't see another option with their natural eyes.

You know, there are a lot of Biblical examples of women who were barren but sought God and received something else instead. Maybe they didn't seek exactly what they hoped for, but they received a blessing that was just for them, working for them and purposed for them. This is all because they sought God and put Him first and allowed Him to fill her in the way that was right for her. If we are willing to do this, God will do for us beyond anything we ask for or imagine.

Seek first the Kingdom

I think women today are afraid to let go of cultural notions and follow God because of where it may take them. I meet a lot of women who try to mix both ideals and while it may seem to work for a time, it winds up not working out in the long run, not with either set of ideals. We are afraid to give up the benefits we seek in the world and too many women think they can hold on to what they want in this world and receive from God, too. It just doesn't work that way.

Matthew 6:33:

But seek ye first the Kingdom of God, and His righteousness; and all these things shall be added unto you. (KJV)

We hear this verse in songs, we hear it preached from the pulpit, we say it, we think on it...and when it comes to doing it, it seems very difficult for us to follow through. If we are to be honest with ourselves, it is a precept that is probably very difficult to live consistently throughout life.

We are commanded to seek first the Kingdom of God and His righteousness before we seek anything else in our lives. This includes the things we want, the things we think we can't live without, and the genuine things that we really need. It is literally that transitional process between delighting ourselves in the Lord and receiving the desires of our heart. The things that we long for should be so bound and hidden in God, that they are His literal will for us and our lives. We can't have it all, especially in the spiritual realm, and especially with one foot in the world and one foot in the Kingdom.

God is calling us to learn what seeking Him truly means. It means trusting everything to Him, emptying ourselves of the world and the needs and cares of this world and trusting Him to fill us and our lives with exactly what will not only bless us, but others through us.

A promise that lasts forever

Luke 2:36-38:

There was also a prophet, Anna, the daughter of Phanuel, of the tribe of Asher. She was very old; she had lived with her husband seven years after her marriage, and then was a widow until she was eighty-four. She never left the temple but worshiped night and day, fasting and praying. Coming up to them at that very moment, she gave thanks to God and spoke about the child to all who were looking forward to the redemption of Jerusalem.

A seldom-studied Biblical woman, the Prophet Anna was an example of a barren woman who emptied herself of much of this world. She had no husband, no children, and spent her entire life in the temple, day and night. She fasted and prayed constantly, because she knew something was coming that she had to be ready to receive.

Anna was barren in every possible sense of the word. Some probably looked at her with pity, as if her life was without meaning or purpose. Barren naturally, she was spiritually alive, aware and pregnant with the Spirit unto the birthing of spiritual greatness. She knew Jesus when she saw Him, and she was the first to tell everyone about what she had seen, announcing the Christ-child was born, alive, and now dedicated in the temple. Even though Simeon, who was also there, had a great revelation and spoke powerful prophetic words, we have no record that he told anyone about it. Anna was so excited; she couldn't keep it to herself. That is the power of a barren woman filled with God!

The power and importance and, yes, blessing, of a barren woman lived in Anna. It lived in many Biblical women, all of whom were ready to be filled with something supernatural. Does that promise live within us today? Does it live within you?

Reflections

- What have you heard in church about barren women?

- How does the teaching on the barren woman make you feel about yourself?

- How can you relate to the barren woman and barren women in the Bible, and what we know about them?

CHAPTER EIGHT

The Christian Woman
- Blessed are the Believers -

AND HE SAITH UNTO ME, WRITE, BLESSED ARE THEY WHICH ARE CALLED UNTO THE MARRIAGE SUPPER OF THE LAMB. AND HE SAITH UNTO ME, THESE ARE THE TRUE SAYINGS OF GOD.
(REVELATION 19:9, KJV)

EVERY week or so, I release a meme on social media with a quotation from a message, book, or something I'm known for saying. It's designed to keep followers connected, giving them something to think about. It's important that we, as Christians, begin to look at our faith in differents way so we can grow spiritually. Not too long ago, in honor of International Women's Day, I posted the following:

"I don't intend to crack the glass ceiling for women in ministry. I intend to burst through it so that no future female generation must believe that all things are possible...unless you are female."

I didn't get a lot of feedback from the post, which surprised me. The quote is from a book I am working on, which I will diligently work on to complete later this year. The point of the quotation, while it spoke of things about women in ministry, was to make us think about the way we tend to approach faith differently for men than we do for women. It's a foregone conclusion that all things are possible to male believers. The world is put at their feet: they are encouraged to be successful; they can be anything they want to be, they can preach, they can run the church, and they can hold positions of leadership. When we start talking about women, however, we don't tend to talk about things like this in the same affirmative fashion. Women are told about specified roles, that they should be satisfied with cultural and social limitations and not try to change them, about being wives and mothers, about how they dress, and about all the things they are "not allowed" to do: preach, teach, minister, hold positions of leadership, run the church, wear certain attire, aspire to success...and the list goes on and on. Women are given the definitive message, in not so few words but through many words, that while all things might be possible with God, they are certainly not possible for them.

The last woman we are looking at in this book is the Christian woman. Even though there is nothing that specifically separates Christian women and blesses them over anyone else who is of a differing gender, I think it's important for us to look at those blessings as applicable to us, as women, as much as they do to anyone else. For whatever reason, the church has become very male in its dominion and motivation, and we are often given the message that women aren't quite as "saved" or as holy as men are. The implication is often made that women don't receive the same promises as men, but that we somehow need to follow men into the Kingdom and then absorb the promises through them, receiving them from a secondary position. The message takes on many forms: out-of-balance teachings on submission, obedience, and aspiration that are all geared to create a certain structure and endorsement between men and women. It might not be a message that a leader even intends to give to a congregation or to the women in that church, but it is one given, loud and clear, many times over.

In my many years as a Christian, a woman, and a minister, I can tell repeated stories where men in ministry tell women in ministry that they can't pursue their ministries or go any further in that work until their husbands "get behind" what they are doing or "get on board" with things. Now, a man in ministry can have a house in total chaos and disorder. Unbiblical as this is, they are encouraged and told to persevere where a woman in the same situation will be quickly thwarted. We need to remember that as women, whether in ministry or not, our salvation does not come through man, but through Christ. We can have a relationship, a calling, and a purpose with God through Christ whether we have a man in our lives, or not.

It's important for us to understand that we are blessed in the Christian life, just as much as men are, walking alongside − not below, behind, or beneath. What's more, we need to walk in these blessings and embrace them as our own, seeing the truth of all God has for us and desires for us.

Being born again

We talked about the new birth some in the last chapter. For such an important Biblical topic, we tell people how to receive it, but we don't teach a lot about it. This has led to all sorts of different interpretations about spiritual life as a Christian, with much confusion about blessing, what it looks like, and how it manifests for the Christian.

Let's say outright: Life in the Kingdom of God is not always easy. I believe our relationship with God and the insights we gain as we go through things and overcome every time compensates for the difficulties we go through. Even in the Kingdom, Jesus tells us there are certain blessings reserved for those who walk in certain Kingdom precepts and abide by certain characteristics. This means Kingdom blessings are reserved for those who are willing to truly walk in the Kingdom way and move from just being someone who is dodging hell to truly becoming a new creature in Christ.

Ephesians 1:3-14:

Blessed be the God and Father of our Lord Jesus Christ, Who hath blessed us with all spiritual blessings in heavenly places in Christ:

According as He hath chosen us in Him before the foundation of the world, that we should be holy and without blame before Him in love:

Having predestinated us unto the adoption of children by Jesus Christ to Himself, according to the good pleasure of His will,

To the praise of the glory of His grace, wherein He hath made us accepted in the beloved.

In Whom we have redemption through His blood, the forgiveness of sins, according to the riches of his grace;

Wherein He hath abounded toward us in all wisdom and prudence;

Having made known unto us the mystery of His will, according to His good pleasure which He hath purposed in Himself:

That in the dispensation of the fulness of times He might gather together in one all things in Christ, both which are in heaven, and which are on earth; even in Him:

In Whom also we have obtained an inheritance, being predestinated according to the purpose of Him Who worketh all things after the counsel of His own will:

That we should be to the praise of His glory, who first trusted in Christ.

In Whom ye also trusted, after that ye heard the word of truth, the gospel of your salvation: in Whom also after that ye believed, ye were sealed with that Holy Spirit of promise,

Which is the earnest of our inheritance until the redemption of the purchased possession, unto the praise of His glory. (KJV)

2 Corinthians 5:16-17:

So from now on we don't think of anyone from a human point of view. If we did think of Christ from a human point of view, we don't anymore. Whoever is a believer in Christ is a new creation. The old way of living has disappeared. A new way of living has come into existence. (GW)

What do these verses teach us? Many people don't become the new creature because they refuse to work out their salvation with fear and trembling. They expect comfort and ease, and when they encounter trials and difficulties, they refuse to see the hope and blessing contained within them. They remain the "old man," with all of their ways and feelings, and then gloss the old person and the old person-nature over with Jesus. Then Jesus gets the blame for their behavior, or how He's not "working" things out as fast as someone else might like...all of which is nothing more than a bunch of excuses for bad behavior.

One of the greatest blessings of the Christian life is transformation. We are not called to have all the same problems, behaviors, challenges, and misdeeds as we did before we were born again. Being born again means just what it says – we start again and are born into a new life and new precepts, and it means we play by new rules. That the blessings of such are reserved for those who really to make the effort to work with the work of salvation God is doing within them and put aside the flesh and walk in the Spirit.

Many presume salvation is all about God because it isn't about our good works. We forget that God doesn't force us to be saved. The work of salvation and the blessing that it brings to us is still something we must choose to receive in our lives. We must also choose to cooperate with it. Those who don't cooperate with God can't expect to receive His benefits. No, that's not about the precept of works versus faith, but about working with God unto the end of the work He is doing within us.

Welcome to the Kingdom

The Beatitudes are among the most well-known and oft-quoted teachings of Jesus. A part of the Sermon on the Mount, they are popular features for posters, samplers, embroidered pillows, pins and T-shirts. It's great to see these things and be reminded of them, but I think we must remember that having them on a pillow or a shirt doesn't mean we understand them or are applying them to our lives. There is extensive blessing present in the Beatitudes. Because we don't really hear enough teaching on them, it's not uncommon to be confused about the precepts they contain.

The word "beatitude" means "blessing." The Beatitudes themselves reflect blessing, lifestyle, and important things that are the result of spiritual mindset. There are specific, special blessings and inheritances reserved for those who exemplify the characteristics, character, and behavior present in these promises. Being a Christian in a true and transforming way – a way that witnesses to others – is not just about what we believe, but also about how we carry ourselves, esteem ourselves, how we act, and what we do. The Beatitudes prove this to us.

Matthew 5:1-3:

Now when Jesus saw the crowds, He went up on a mountainside and sat down. His disciples came to Him, and He began to teach them.

He said:

"Blessed are the poor in spirit,
for theirs is the Kingdom of heaven.

- **Blessed are the poor in spirit, for theirs is the Kingdom of heaven**: By definition, such are those who know they need God and recognize they can't live without Him. This passage isn't saying people are poor in their amount of the Spirit, but are poor in spirit, which means they recognize in and of themselves they have nothing without God. As we learned in the last chapter, what happens to those who pursue God – they receive the Kingdom of Heaven, because the Kingdom is for such who have become humble enough to find God and realize it's not all about them. This is a far bigger deal then we would like to consider, because many people in this world never come to the humbling realization that they need God in a way that can transform and bring them to a new place in Him.

Receiving the Kingdom is a primary Kingdom benefit. It's our inheritance, and one often easily promoted and published to others. Come and receive the Kingdom! We tell others they will receive it when they die, but we don't recognize the Kingdom inheritance must benefit now as much as later. If the Kingdom of heaven belongs to us, that means we receive it now. It is received this side of heaven through faith, and living by Kingdom precepts and benefits, acknowledging its rule and purpose in this world, and walking in the joy, love and peace of the Holy Ghost all make the Kingdom alive and purposeful, a blessed and satisfying experience.

Matthew 5:4-7:

Blessed are those who mourn,
* for they will be comforted.*
Blessed are the meek,
* for they will inherit the earth.*
Blessed are those who hunger and thirst for
* righteousness,*
* for they will be filled.*
Blessed are the merciful,

for they will be shown mercy.

- **Blessed are those who mourn, for they will be comforted:** Mourning is a sign of true contrition; a turning of heart, if you will. Mourning, however, is not just reserved for realization of one's personal sins. We see in the life of Jeremiah a man who, as part of his prophetic call, walked in weeping and sorrow for the sins of his generation and the nation of Israel at large. It is possible to stand beside or aside and mourn for the sins of a generation or lost souls, or anything else. It is not just about being sorry for what one has done personally. When one mourns, they mourn for anything that one knows grieves God, and therefore, it grieves the individual who has the heart of God, as well.

  This also causes us to stand and realize there is something sincere in the process of spiritual realization, something that causes us to see things differently and invites divine comfort and healing to an individual. When we grieve, God steps in and offers us a spiritual respite that only He can provide.

  How many of us can truly say what we see causes us "grief unto mourning?" There's a lot of things in this world that don't disturb us enough when we hear about them. We might be quick to mourn if something affects us personally, especially if it hits home at our family, personal finances, or comfort zone. We can see a thousand pictures of starving children with no shoes, watch the horrors of a school shooting on television, or hear about women dying in childbirth, but we aren't moved nearly enough because it has nothing to do with us (or so we think). We should be far more grieved and move to intercede on behalf of whatever it is we see, much more often than we do.

The blessing one receives for righteous mourning is comfort. Knowing that God is with the individual and that He does forgive repentant sins as well as hear true intercessory cries is a powerful thing to witness in the life of a blessed Christian. We also discover that God is in control, and we live to see prayers answered and God resolve situations.

I meet a lot of people who claim to be intercessors, but I believe the true test of an intercessor is the awareness one has, especially of the sinful state of humanity. Their personal level of mourning for the results of sin and its impact on life's circumstances measure how serious one is about wrangling between heaven and earth. Mourning doesn't mean we make a spectacle of ourselves, as some who claim to be intercessors do. It's not cute to throw yourself all over the altar in your prayer shawl, making sure everyone sees and knows what's happening. It does mean we take to heart the things that are sinful or painful, and we don't make light of such. In seeing the natural pains of humanity, we offer spiritual aid to them.

- **Blessed are the meek, for they will inherit the earth**: We often mistake meekness for weakness. Meekness is not weakness. Meekness is humility in that we empty ourselves and allow the character and nature that God wills for us to have to take over our lives. It respects the ability to manage power through self-control and allowing ourselves to be divinely led into all truth through our character as much as what we believe. Meekness puts aside what we want. In it, we are humble enough to accept and desire what God wants for us more than what we want ourselves. Meekness is squarely that emptying of self and acceptance of divine will.

To receive the earth as an inheritance means all that will be in the new earth will be theirs. The earth will become a place of their own authority and dominion, to educate and judge along with God. Why does this go to the meek? Because they are do not look at people or things from a worldly perspective. When we stand back and observe things from a worldly perspective, we don't see God's perspective (too many things cloud our judgment)s. Meekness allows a necessary shift in perspective to focus on heavenly things, and gives a great perspective to lead and rule.

- **Blessed are those who hunger and thirst for righteousness, for they will be filled**: Are you truly hungry and thirsty for right things? Those who do so live to partake and be filled with righteousness in their very being, as their very sustenance. They desire to receive it and it be the very state and ability to live and operate. They desire righteousness – right standing with God, right actions with others, right nature in character – a full package of living a testament of righteousness is what they want to take in, because it is exactly who they want to be.

  People who long for righteousness want it within themselves so they can give it to others. Sometimes we forget about the need to do right both by and for others, because down the line, the world will end anyway. This is the wrong view. We should long for right so much, doing right and drawing to right becomes second nature. Christians should desire to transform things with the love of God, seeking to do them whether it changes the life of one person or the life of millions of people.

  God will fulfill this desire. Those who seek righteousness will receive the total and complete righteousness they seek. As they continue in it, they will attain it and will impact the lives of others because of it.

- **Blessed are the merciful, for they will be shown mercy**: This beatitude expresses a basic purpose and condition for our faith: those who show mercy (kindness, compassion, empathy, and unmerited understanding) in a situation will, in turn, receive it. God Himself has mercy on us. We walk in this fact because we know God does not have to be merciful to us, but He chooses mercy out of His great love for us. Mercy is, in a sense, love in action: it does not enable, but it recognizes a divine precept that we can't pretend does not exist. A tangible aspect of God's forgiveness, mercy transforms everything it touches.

We know if we are merciful to others, God shows us an even greater mercy in our own shortcomings. This is self-awareness and humility. In mercy, we realize that much of what others to do us is validly upsetting...but we often do the same, if not similar things, in a different form ourselves. I know we like to super-spiritualize things sometimes, but I believe mercy is, in its very essence, a patient love wrought in understanding as people work out their faults with God and one another. It acknowledges the process people go through, where they will hopefully wind up, and where they are going. It looks at situations not from the flesh, but with the heart of God in mind.

Understanding true character

Matthew 5:8-9

Blessed are the pure in heart,
 for they will see God.
Blessed are the peacemakers,

for they will be called children of God.

- **Blessed are the pure in heart, for they will see God**: The Bible speaks about the importance of being pure, to the end of saying that to those who are pure, all things are pure. Even though we tend to use the term "purity" in the sense of abstaining from sex, this isn't really what the Bible is talking about. A pure heart bespeaks of intentions that we can't always see on the surface. If someone is pure, their intentions and motives are both right and honorable. There is nothing covert, nor secretive, within them.

  Pure hearts are uncomfortable with sin and do their best to avoid acquaintance with it. They don't deliberately act in sin, nor use sinfulness as a motive for action. We should all work with the motivation to be pure in heart: to have nothing to do with a wrong spirit or acting vengeful.

  Perhaps more than anything, being pure in heart means one is authentic and honest in who they are. They aren't trying to put on airs or appear one way to impress other people. Purity is next to sincerity, which works in cooperation to create trustworthiness in an individual.

  The blessing for the pure at heart is to see God Himself. Sin cannot stand in the presence of God. If we are to be in His presence and see Him as He is, we cannot walk in or operate with sin as our motivation. I believe it also sees God for God, not through the reflective lens where God appears to be nothing more than a big version of us, magnifying ourselves.

  Pureness of heart doesn't just refrain from sin. It also refuses to let sin permeate one's life. We tend to tolerate things we shouldn't and look the other way in the name of fitting in, being polite, not offending others, or maintaining a status quo of life we would rather not disturb...so we compromise. We need to stop tolerating the sin done to us, around us, or that we ourselves inflict in the name of keeping our friends, relationships, and status quo around us. Instead, we need to seek first the Kingdom and trust that God will add all those blessed things to us, because we don't compromise ourselves in the name of holding onto things in our lives.

- **Blessed are the peacemakers, for they will be called sons of God**: The peace spoken of here is more than that which we see in the temporal world. Obviously, it is a good thing to work for peace and promote peace between nations or seek an end to war. Political peace is a great and important thing to which all nations should aspire. War and battles between and within nations are terrible things. Those who pay dearly for the spoils of war are average citizens, people who want to live, you guessed it − in some semblance of peace. But being a peacemaker is about bring peace to each and every situation in one's life. It's not attempting to be a peacekeeper (by which you don't say anything in order to keep a status quo in place), but being someone radical enough to recognize peace, wholeness, and completeness are the same thing, and they need to manifest in every situation, everywhere you go.

Being a peacemaker means being a bearer of Christ: carrying the ultimate blessing of good news and grace in every situation. We do not stir nor agitate with every situation, feeling, or circumstance that comes along. We remain constant and focused and are not easily distracted or disturbed.

Peacemakers are called the children of God because they know the inheritance they have through the work of peace. The devil, people, circumstances, and issues of life don't distract them. They are not ruled by things that aren't their problem. They don't listen to gossip, follow the teachings of false leaders, and they know how to mind their own business. Thus, being called a "child of God" is truly an incredible blessing. In this state, one is spiritually begotten of God and ready to move with God, in peace, not the world, at any given time.

Matthew 5:10:

Blessed are those who are persecuted because of righteousness,
for theirs is the Kingdom of heaven.

- **Blessed are those who are persecuted because of righteousness, for theirs is the Kingdom of heaven**: Here we are going to talk about something we don't talk enough about in church, and that is persecution for true righteousness' sake. Those who do right, and experience persecution, gain unique spiritual perspective and growth. It provides insight they can't get from something else in life. As inheritors of the Kingdom, they see the Kingdom with an appreciation because it offers them the peace and love that they long for, but do not find, in this world.

  In western society, we often confuse persecution with not getting our own way in a social or political context. For example, there are many situations where secular employers are brought into court for discriminating against someone with different beliefs, and the business owner cries discrimination. They claim their Christian beliefs are being violated. This is not persecution. If you don't

BLESSED THOUGHTS:

The song of the strong woman

I once was weak but now am strong. I have been strengthened in Him. I have made my bad choices, I have lived with the consequences, as did the generations of women before me. I know my heritage. We have done what we needed to do and were who we needed to be. We have lived with the abuse, the fear, the terror, the burdens, and somehow, we have all stood firm to come to today. I draw on my heritage. I draw on my mothers in biology, in spirit, in faith, and in history. They have run my race; and I now run theirs. We were once weak, and now we are strong. We are strong because we have to be, because God has made us to be strong.

I draw on my heritage; on my spiritual mothers: Deborah, Mary, Esther, Vashti, Ruth, Naomi, Abigail, Junia, Apphia, Photini, Sarah, the woman with the issue of blood, Salome, Mary Magdalene, Elizabeth, Jael, Hannah, the daughters of Job, Lois, Eunice, Priscilla, Jephthah's daughter, the daughters of Zelophehad, Eve, Rebecca, Anna, the daughters of Philip, and the many others who are our matriarchs in the faith. We have our role models. Society has sanitized them and made them nothing more than slaves to men, but they were so much more than that. They belonged to God, not to men. They were strong because they had to be. They had to confront their times and their lives. They brought change and challenge. They were strong because God made them that way. They were unashamed of the strength God gave them. I stand unashamed of the strength God gave me.

I know my voice. I know my Father's voice. I am His, and He is mine. In Him, I have the strength that I need to speak the words He gives to me. I am free to speak my mind. I do not need to apologize for being strong. I do not need to apologize for speaking my mind.

I am not always sweet. As a strong woman, people may never see me as sweet...and that is fine with me. People want me to be sweet. Men want me to be sweet. Men want me to be "nice." They want me to sit down and be quiet. They do not want to be challenged; to be confronted, they want me to be silent unless it is to praise what they do. I am not sweet. I do not placate. I am strong and I tell it like it is. I do not always speak perfectly, but I always speak truthfully. Truth is not always sweet nor is it nice, but it sets us free. To be strong, I had to accept the truth about myself. I had to accept my limitations, my excelling, who I was, and who I wanted to be. In doing so, it set me free so I could stand strong.

When I say you were disrespectful, it is because you were disrespectful...it is not because I was "emotionally hurt" by someone else. When I talk to you, I am talking to you. I am not talking to my father, my ex-boyfriend, my ex-husband, my husband, my brother, my mother, my sister, my friend, or anyone else in my life. I do not need to be patronized. I know the difference between concern and condescending. I didn't once, but I do now, because now I am strong. Some days we need a hug, some days we need to talk, some days we need to be left alone. I know how I feel; I don't need to be told how to feel. Strong women feel and go through and most of the world never knows because they keep going and keep getting stronger.

I am in touch with myself and my tastes. I know who I am in Christ. With Him living in me, I am holy. Holiness is not how I wear my hair, how long my skirt is, what color my dress is, whether or not I wear pants, whether or not I wear make-up, whether or not I dye my hair, whether or not I can drive a car, what my last name is, whose house I live in, whether or not I wear jewelry, whether or not I have a job, whether or not I am married or have children; holiness is who I am in Christ.

I am lonely at times, but never alone. Eagles fly alone, and we must sometimes make decisions that mean we stand alone, too. Strong women pay the price of non-dependency; we are free but live in a bound world. Worldly relationships are built on dependencies and needs and people needing each other, rather than choosing each other. I choose who is in my life; I choose to love those who are around me and receive love in return. I do not need a relationship to validate my existence, because my relationship with God already does that for me. I am empowered by the Holy Spirit, God working in my experience, both spiritual and practical.

I am at peace with who I am. I spent years trying to be what others called me to be or what they thought I should be. I am not what others think I am; I am what God thinks I am. That makes me different. I don't fit in a box; I am not always neat; I do not always color in the lines. I did not always understand. It is not always comfortable to be different. People do not always agree; they do not always respect; they do not always understand. But this is who I am. It has taken me a long time for me to get here. No matter what you may think of me, I cannot change for another person.

I am an example. The Lord has set me as a sign to others of what can happen when we are in Him. I am not where I used to be anymore. I am not that person. I remember her, I felt her pain, I lived with her hurts and her fears, but I am not her now. I am a new creature because He has made me new, and I am in Him.

I am strong for a purpose. I cannot be like everyone else, which is why He has made me strong. In my strength, I sing the Lord's song and rejoice in His battle cry. The cycle goes on as I continue in Him; from my strength, other women know too that God calls them to be strong.

follow the law and do not treat people with common dignity or respect, you are going to face certain legal ramifications for such behavior. Is it uncomfortable, sure, but it should challenge those in these circumstances to stretch their faith and become better believers.

There are people in this world who are genuinely persecuted for their faith in Christ. There are several countries where being a Christian is illegal, and being found with things such as Bibles or crosses can land someone in prison or worse. Christians are killed, lose their housing, jobs, suffer reproach among families, lose custody of their children, go to jail, or are killed, all in pursuit of the life of the Kingdom. They are blessed for this because they acknowledge with their own lives that the Kingdom is first and is more important to them than whatever they might have to give up in the meantime. They are willing to pay a price that many are simply unwilling to pay, and that renders unto them a special blessing.

Being blessed, but hated

Matthew 5:11-12:

Blessed are you when people insult you, persecute you and falsely say all kinds of evil against you because of Me. Rejoice and be glad, because great is your reward in heaven, for in the same way they persecuted the prophets who were before you.

- **Blessed are you when people insult you, persecute you and falsely say all kinds of evil against you because of Me**: Here, we see another blessing that comes from persecution, insult, and false words spoken against believers. The Christian life is spoken nowhere in the Bible (or out of the Bible) as being easy. The truth is that the world (and when I say the "world," I mean the system that exists in the world that is opposed to the righteousness of God) hates what it doesn't understand. The Christian life – the true Christian life – is one that is not well understood by the world.

  Being a Christian woman brings special consideration to what we are discussing: What God calls us to pursue and the priorities He calls us to have are different from those the world encourages us to pursue. The world is not going to react kindly to those who literally proclaim that it has absolutely no purpose and that no good shall come from following its precepts. The call to be and live different, especially as a woman, will bear special hostilities with it.

  What we bear in His Name is blessed because we do it for Him. We are a people that are blessed but hated much of the time. Some people don't decide they want to follow Christ when they see what we have received from Him. They get angry because they don't want to do or go through what we've had to do or go through to receive that blessing in our lives. They make life hard for us, hoping what we have will be taken away. We know, though, that just because they make life hard doesn't mean that anyone can take it away!

- **Rejoice and be glad, because great is your reward in heaven, for in the same way they persecuted the prophets who were before you**: Our greatest reward and blessing lie in heaven. This doesn't mean we have to wait until death to see it, but some of the benefits of Kingdom living we will not see now. We will see them one day, when God appoints them to us, after the spiritual and natural realms change. Regardless, we are called to rejoice in these times! We are in touch with our heritage as Christian believers, because those who have stood for what is true have always paid a heavy price. The prophets didn't have it easy, but they persevered on because they believed in God, what He stood for, and that they would see a better, blessed day.

It's important we think on these things and recognize being Christian women is something truly out of this world: different, radical, outrageous, and powerful. It comes with its own benefits and blessings, which as we adopt the nature of Christ, we can walk in and receive in greater abundance.

Walking in principle that reaps an eternal harvest

Matthew 5:13-16

You are the salt of the earth. But if the salt loses its saltiness, how can it be made salty again? It is no longer good for anything, except to be thrown out and trampled by men.

You are the light of the world. A town built on a hill cannot be hidden. Neither do people light a lamp and put it under a bowl. Instead the put it on its stand, and it gives light to everyone in the house. In the same way, let your light shine before others, that they may see your good deeds and glorify your Father in heaven.

After we hear about these blessings of believers, we receive a command repeated in a couple of different ways, told through stories so they will be understandable to those who receive them. The command to be salt, light, and a city on the hill comes after these other characteristics that reap blessing, which tells us something important. We are to walk in the characteristics mentioned here, not just for the purpose of getting blessed and receiving benefits, but for the greater purpose of glorifying God.

God has bestowed much within us as Christian women. We are special; we are unique; we are His daughters; and we are here, now, to be His chosen vessels of change in the world. Our ultimate purpose in walking through what God has for us and the blessings He has for us is to bring glory not for us, but unto Him.

In summary...A man can't do a woman's job, no matter how hard he tries. Only you can be God's woman, most blessed among all women.

Reflections

- When you read the Beatitudes, where do you fit into the picture?

- What does seeing these different characteristics and blessings make you want to do the same? Do differently?

- What is God calling you to do as a woman of God in your life?

CONCLUSION

You are Most Blessed!

GOD WANTED TO MAKE VERY CLEAR [DEMONSTRATE CONVINCINGLY]
TO THOSE WHO WOULD GET WHAT HE PROMISED [THE HEIRS OF THE PROMISE]
THAT HIS PURPOSES [OR PLANS] NEVER CHANGE,
SO HE MADE [CONFIRMED/GUARANTEED IT WITH] AN OATH.
(HEBREWS 6:17, EXB)

YEARS ago, Kermit the Frog told us, "It's not easy being green." The song shared how, within Kermit's experience, having to be the way he was throughout his life was not easy for him. At the same time, even though it was hard, it wasn't all bad to be green. Green didn't just mean he camouflaged well. It also meant he was cool and friendly, and there were things about being green that others associated with likable and essential qualities.

I think being a woman is often like Kermit's experience. Sometimes it feels like we are lost, invisible, unable to be seen or heard, and that we are just blending in with the rest of the world. We feel unimportant, unnoticed, uncared about, unappreciated, and yes, unblessed. We watch as others are selected instead of us, and we feel ignored and passed over as life passes us by.

God doesn't desire that our entire lives pass us by as

we feel bad about "being green" or going unnoticed. We are all unique, created with our own set of circumstances, attributes, abilities, and God-given purposes. There might be times when our lives are quieter than others or more unknown than someone else's life, but there will always be a point where God will put us, front and center, to shine His light to a lost and hurting world. We must be willing to step out from the shadows and out from the places where women are known to stay and be societally comfortable. We must be willing to do something different, coming out from the places we have been told to stay and do the things we have always done...and come into our own springtime, where we are noticed.

You, woman of God, are most blessed. It might not feel that way. It might not always look that way. It might not always be exactly what you expected it to be, but you are most blessed. You are most blessed because you are you and there is no one else quite like you who can do just what God has asked you to do. You, woman of God, are special. It's time to rise above fear, rise above expectation, rise above anxiety, rise above the angers, pursuits, and hostilities of the flesh, and move to a new day. God, the One Who loves you more than anything: your Father, your Friend, your spiritual Husband, your Leader, your Love, and your Truth is calling to you to come to Him, just as you are, and discover the wonder that He has placed in you. Respond to that call. Answer that call. Be the change you wish to see in the world. Rest in Him, and find everything you have always wanted, as He blesses you beyond every imaginable measure.

Push through to your purpose...your outrageously blessed, empowered, and sacred life.

References

[1] <u>Strong's Exhaustive Concordance of the Bible</u>, #3107

[2] Information from: "Rubies."
https://en.wikipedia.org/wiki/Ruby. Accessed May 23, 2009.

[3] "Barrenness." http://www.merriam-webster.com/dictionary/barrenness. Accessed April 14, 2016.

ABOUT THE AUTHOR

Dr. Lee Ann B. Marino, Ph.D., D.Min., D.D.

THESE THAT HAVE TURNED THE WORLD UPSIDE DOWN ARE COME HITHER ALSO.
(ACTS 17:6, KJV)

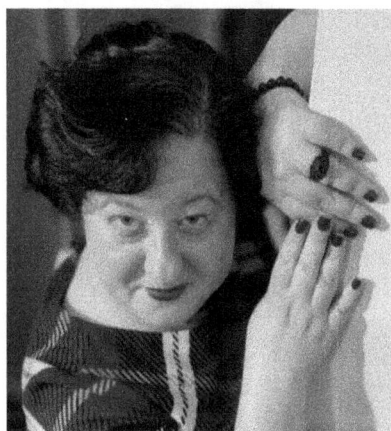

Dr. Lee Ann B. Marino, Ph.D., D.Min., D.D. (she/her) is "everyone's favorite theologian" leading Gen X, Millennials, and Gen Z with expertise in leadership training, queer and feminist theology, general religion, and apostolic theology. She has served in ministry since 1998 and was ordained as a pastor in 2002 and an apostle in 2010. She founded what is now Sanctuary Apostolic Fellowship Empowerment (SAFE) Ministries in 2004. Under her ministry heading Dr. Marino is founder and Overseer of Sanctuary International Fellowship Tabernacle (SIFT) (the original home of National Coming Out Sunday) and The Sanctuary Network, and Chancellor of Apostolic Covenant Theological Seminary (ACTS).

Affectionately nicknamed "the Spitfire," Dr. Marino has spent over two decades as an "apostle, preacher, and teacher" (2 Timothy 1:11), exercising her personal mandate to become "all things to all people" (1 Corinthians 9:22). Her embrace of spiritual issues (both technical and intimate) has found its home among both seekers and believers, those who desire spiritual answers to today's issues.

Dr. Marino has preached throughout the United States, Puerto Rico, and Europe in hundreds of religious services and experiences throughout the years. A history maker in her own right, she has spent over two decades in advocacy, education, and work for and within minority spiritual communities (including African American, Hispanic, and LGBTQ+). She has also served as the first woman on all-male synods, councils, and panels, as well as the first preacher or speaker welcomed of a different race, sexual orientation, or identity among diverse communities. Today, Dr. Marino's work extends to over 150 countries as she hosts the popular *Kingdom Now* podcast, which is in the top 20 percentile of all podcasts worldwide. She is also the author of over 35 books and the popular Patheos column, *Leadership on Fire*. To date, she has had five bestselling titles within their subject matter: *Understanding Demonology, Spiritual Warfare, Healing, and Deliverance: A Manual for the Christian Minister; Ministry School Boot Camp: Training for Helps Ministries, Appointments, and Beyond; Discovering Intimacy: A Journey Through the Song of Solomon; Fruit of the Vine: Study and Commentary on the Fruit of the Spirit;* and *Ministering to LGBTQ+ (and Those Who Love Them): A Primer for Queer Theology* (and its accompanying workbook).

As a public icon and social media influencer, Dr. Marino advocates healthy body image (curvy/full-figured), representation as a demisexual/aromantic, and albinism awareness as a model. Known to those she works with, she is a spiritual mom, teacher, leader, professor, confidant, and friend. She continues to transform, receiving new teaching, revelation, and insight in this thing we call "ministry." Through years of spiritual growth and maturity, Dr. Marino stands as herself, here to present what God has given to her for any who have an ear to hear.

For more information, visit her website at kingdompowernow.org.

www.ingramcontent.com/pod-product-compliance
Lightning Source LLC
Chambersburg PA
CBHW060155070426
42447CB00033B/1477